# A
## THE

PAN BOOKS

First published 1992 by True Crime Library

This edition published 2005 by Pan Books
an imprint of Pan Macmillan Ltd
Pan Macmillan, 20 New Wharf Road, London N1 9RR
Basingstoke and Oxford
Associated companies throughout the world
www.panmacmillan.com

ISBN 0 330 42113 1

1 3 5 7 9 8 6 4 2

A CIP catalogue record for this book is available from
the British Library.

Printed and bound in Great Britain by
Mackays of Chatham plc, Chatham, Kent

To the victims and
families of victims
who died by the
hand of a murderer

# CONTENTS

# PREFACE

It's one of the oddities of life that murder, the most serious crime in the calendar, is normally committed by amateurs. True, a few hit-men, a few gangsters, a few bank robbers muscle in on the act from time to time. But the fact remains that over ninety per cent of murderers are amateurs. Many of them, prior to that one act of madness, have led perfectly blameless lives. And few will have given themselves any real chance of escaping the consequences of their act.

As a prison officer, I have come into contact with many murderers. I have studied them at close range; and yet found it impossible to establish any common thread. Look at them and you'll realise that outwardly at least they're very much like you and me. You will find their counterparts on any street . . . that jolly chap who lives next door . . . the timid little librarian with her shy smile . . . the henpecked husband down the road . . . the eternal mother surrounded by her adoring brood . . . and so on.

This is the terrifying part of it. If all murderers looked like monsters, they'd be easy to spot and we'd be on our guard. It's their guise of normality which is so alarming. After all, the residents of Rillington Place were astonished when John Reginald Christie was charged with murder. They were convinced that there had been a mistake. They just couldn't bring themselves to believe that this mild, bespectacled little man could have been a mass killer, filling his cupboards with corpses. And over and over again, you get this reaction after an arrest for murder. Total disbelief from friends, workmates and neighbours alike.

So inevitably we have to ask ourselves the question . . . is it possible that we are all capable of murder? Could it be that ever since Adam and Eve, the seeds of violence and mayhem have been implanted in the human heart . . . that we are all walking time bombs, some more explosive than others . . . that given a certain set of circumstances, we could all squeeze the trigger and happily wipe a fellow human being off the face of the earth?

If I knew all the answers to the above, I probably wouldn't have written this book. Call it, if you like, a search for truth; because I don't believe we can ever hope to cope with crime and the criminal, until we first learn to understand them.

In the pages that follow, you will find some of the murders which have intrigued me most over the years, very often because of their sheer futility. In each case, I focus my attention on the murderer and wonder what devil drove him, or her, along this awful path to self-destruction. For all those featured in this book share a common fate . . . all ending their lives with the hangman's noose around their necks.

For some, you will doubtless wish to shed no tears. But there will be others whom you may feel deserved a kinder fate . . . and a few at least who were in reality victims too. However by the time you reach the final page, I suspect that, like me, you will have found more questions than answers. Murder can be a baffling business.

# 1

# THE ABSENT-MINDED CAPTAIN

*"Well, that's over. I hope my tea won't be late."*
*Frederick (Eric) Rothwell Holt's remark to the*
*prison governor, only seconds after he'd been*
*sentenced to death.*

It had just started to rain as Kitty Breaks stepped on to the sands. But the dark angry sky warned that this was only a prelude to the wildness to come. Already there was the sound of distant thunder. She lifted the collar of her coat, shaking her head as though reprimanding God. But she was smiling, because she liked to feel the rain on her face. On such nights, all her troubles would soon be washed away.

She began to walk along the edge of the sea. It was December, 1919, and Christmas was just three days away. In the distance, she could see the festive lights along the Blackpool front. Fortunately, she had slipped on fleece-lined boots and a thick coat which covered her knees. Even so she shivered a little as the wind lifted the flaps of her coat, placing its cold impudent fingers on the soft warm flesh of her thighs.

The waves were gradually being whipped into a fury and a jagged streak of lightning lit the night sky, followed instantly by a clap of thunder. She looked upwards, once more reprimanding this all-powerful god of the skies . . .

reminding him that she had wanted a soothing string quartet, not a full orchestra with cymbals and drums.

Another streak of lightning spotlighted her face; and lashed by the wind and the rain the face was beautiful, almost pagan in its pleasure. Then suddenly she saw him and pleasure gave way to puzzlement and then to alarm. There was a gun in his hand and it was pointing straight at her.

For a moment, neither of them moved. "Why are you doing this," she cried. "Tell me why."

By way of answer, he slipped back the safety catch and she knew only sudden lurching terror. She opened her mouth to scream or to plead; but before she could do either, the gun exploded and she felt a searing pain below her breast. She fell backwards on to the sands. He stood over her. He stood astride, took aim again and fired two more shots. Then when he was quite sure she was dead, he slipped off his gloves, dropping them beside the body . . . and then, almost as an afterthought, he dropped the gun too.

A fisherman found her body on the sands by the first light of day. The gloves and the gun lay nearby and the killer's footprints were clearly visible. After only the briefest examination, the police were able to rule out both rape and robbery.

They broke the news to her common-law husband, Frederick Rothwell Holt (known as Eric), a former Territorial captain who had served in the trenches during the First World War. After being invalided out of the army, he'd worked in Malaya before returning home to his native Lancashire in 1918.

This was the year in which he'd met the young and beautiful Kitty Breaks. At first, Kitty had presented herself as a single woman; but later confessed that she was very unhappily married and had lived apart from her husband almost since their wedding day. Holt brushed aside this revelation and became her lover. For eighteen months they lived happily together, exchanging tender letters whenever they were apart.

In the terminology of the day, Holt was an officer and a gentleman. The police soon became convinced that he was a murderer too, and they were astonished by his attitude. He appeared to treat the whole matter with indifference. He admitted that the revolver and the gloves found beside the body belonged to him. He also seemed unsurprised by the fact that the shoes he was wearing matched the footprints on the sands; but he still couldn't understand why the police wished to interview him. He was duly arrested and charged.

Holt's trial took place before the mild-mannered and courteous Mr. Justice Greer, while two of the finest advocates of the day sat in opposition. The Attorney General, Sir Gordon Hewart, led for the Crown. And Holt was defended by the legendary Sir Edward Marshall Hall.

Sir Edward and his team decided to raise, as a preliminary issue, the question of "unfit to plead," and a jury was sworn in to decide the matter. Several doctors were convinced that the prisoner was insane. Holt had claimed that he was being visited in his cell by huge American flies carrying fever germs to persecute him and that the police had sent in dogs to unnerve him.

Sir Gordon argued that Holt was making up the story in an attempt to simulate delusional insanity. The jury, after a short retirement, decided that he was fit to plead; and a second jury was then sworn in.

The Crown built up an overwhelming case, putting forward a double motive. Firstly, there was Holt's desire to collect the insurance money on Kitty's life. She had recently insured herself for £5,000 and made a will, leaving everything to Holt. Secondly, it was suggested that he wished to rid himself of an embarrassing liaison . . . in other words, that of living with another man's wife.

"I will not dwell," said Sir Gordon, "on the accumulated evidence. The gloves, his gloves, how did they come to be there? The footprints, his footprints, how did they come to be there? The revolver, his revolver, how did that come to be there too?"

A number of witnesses traced Holt's movements on the day of the murder. He and Kitty had travelled by train from Bradford. Holt left the train at Ansdell station and Kitty had gone on alone to Blackpool. After changing for dinner, she had gone for that wild walk on the sands, setting out alone. Meanwhile Holt had been seen boarding a tram close to the sands between nine and ten that night.

The prosecution case closed on the fourth day of the trial and Sir Edward found himself in something of a dilemma. Since his arrest, Holt had refused to cooperate with his legal advisers, merely stating over and over again that he was innocent.

His behaviour in court had become steadily stranger. He spent much of his time staring into space, seemingly totally uninterested in the trial itself. Dr Blair, who was the senior medical officer at the Lancaster County Asylum, had told the court that Holt's grandfather and a first cousin had been insane. He was certain that Holt suffered from the same delusions as his two relatives. Sir Edward was equally convinced that his client was insane; and felt it quite impossible to put him in the witness box.

If the situation had been different, he might have made great play of the fact that Holt seemingly had an alibi. The whole of his family had given evidence, stating that he was at home with them on the night of the murder. But the man himself was unable to support his own alibi, because he apparently couldn't remember anything at all about that fateful night. It was just a blank in his memory.

Sir Edward's final speech to the jury on the fifth day has been described as the most moving speech of his entire career. He read passages from letters written by Holt and Kitty. He spoke for two hours without referring to a single note. The judge sat with his head bowed and with tears in his eyes, as did most of the jury. The only person in the courtroom who appeared unmoved was Holt himself. He was struggling to read a newspaper with some difficulty. This wasn't really surprising. He was holding it upside down.

The last letter read out by Sir Edward had been written

by Holt a few days before Kitty's death.

> *"My Dear Darling Kathleen (Kitty's real name),*
> *You have no idea how lonely I feel without you,*
> *dearest. I arrived safely tonight, but I did, and do, so*
> *want you nearer to me, you dear, sweet thing. You love*
> *me, I love you. I feel I must always be near you; you*
> *have no idea how I feel after I leave you, or you leave*
> *me, darling. I do so want you to think the same of me. I*
> *am sorry at what happened to us at lunch today, but let*
> *us both forget it, and may neither of us notice such a*
> *thing again. I know we are too fond of each other for*
> *that. I feel you will never leave me after Christmas. I long*
> *for some good Christmases with you in times to come, and*
> *feel that some time there will be no parting us."*

There was a long pause, then Sir Edward said, "How could a man write letters like these, then savagely kill the woman he loved a few days later? I will tell you. A man like the prisoner who has been in France, and subjected to the nerve-racking experience of the Festubert bombardment . . . a man who is neurasthenic, and who has suffered from loss of memory and depression . . . is the very man who might at any moment go mad."

Never before had Sir Edward been moved to such a high pitch of emotion. Sir Gordon's reply, which lasted for three and a half hours, was by contrast cold and deadly.

Mr. Justice Greer's summing-up was spoken in a low, gentle voice. He said, "Strange things happen in human life and it is not impossible that a man might combine with his affection for the woman, feelings which might enable him, when the time was ripe, to commit a crime of this kind."

As to insanity, in 1920 the guidelines were laid down by the McNaghten rules formulated some eighty years previously. Mr. Justice Greer left the question of uncontrollable impulse to the jury, a question not covered by McNaghten. He told the jury that if they came to the conclusion that Holt had committed the murder while under the influence of some uncontrollable impulse, they would have the right to acquit him. He gave the impression that he would be happy if they did.

Nevertheless, after an hour's deliberation, the jury returned a verdict of guilty. As Holt was brought back into court, he was folding and pushing a newspaper into his pocket, seemingly totally unconcerned by the situation. Sir Herbert Stephen, the assize clerk, asked him if he had anything to say before being sentenced. Holt simply shrugged his shoulders and stared at the clock, as though anxious to be gone.

The black cap was placed on the judge's wig and, for the second time during the case, tears poured down his cheeks as he passed the sentence of death.

Holt turned and marched smartly down to the cells and spotting the prison governor, Major Fitzclarence, he spoke for the first time that day. "Well, that's over," he said briskly. "I hope my tea won't be late."

But Sir Edward, convinced that an injustice was being done, hadn't given up. He took the case to the Court of Appeal where the Lord Chief Justice, Lord Reading, gave him permission to produce additional evidence. A Dr Day, who practised in Malaya, realised while reading reports of the trial, that he had treated Holt for syphilis during his stay there. He had telegraphed Sir Edward on the last day of the trial, too late to give evidence.

Sir Edward decided that Dr Day must, if possible, be called for the appeal. When making the application, he said, "I am going to ask your Lordships to consider in 1920 the whole question of insanity and the subject of mental disorders. It is time the question was settled. I am going to show that, owing to a condition of mind which was partly due to heredity and partly to syphilis, the appellant killed Mrs. Breaks as the result of uncontrollable impulse."

Dr Day gave evidence and then Dr Blair from the Lancaster Asylum was called. He said he hadn't known about Holt's syphilis at the trial; but in view of this, he now considered that he had been suffering from general paralysis of the insane at the time of the murder.

All Sir Edward's efforts were in vain. The court decided that the trial judge had quite clearly left the question of uncontrollable impulse to the jury; and that the additional evidence did not warrant any interference with the original verdict.

Lord Reading added that the rules in McNaghten must be observed. It was not sufficient for a medical expert to come forward and say generally that a criminal was insane to warrant a verdict being overturned.

The Home Secretary ordered a special medical enquiry to be made into Holt's state of mind. He then found that he was unable to grant a reprieve and Holt was executed on April 13, 1920.

So died a confused and absent-minded man who, since the death of Kitty Breaks, appeared to have lived in some strange and lonely world of his own.

There can be little doubt that he killed her. But would a sane man have left his gun and gloves beside the body? And having made the footprints, would a sane man still continue to wear the same shoes on the following day?

Two questions remain unanswered.

Why did Kitty go for a walk on that wild and windy night? She was known to be a girl who believed in walking away her troubles. So what was troubling her that night? Could it have been that she sensed her lover was going mad?

And the biggest question of all: why did he shoot her? In view of the overwhelming evidence, the Crown didn't need to establish a motive; and the two suggested must be regarded as little more than shots in the dark. Certainly in view of the letters read out in court, it is difficult to believe that he was overly concerned with either the insurance money or an embarrassing liaison. During one of Holt's rare moments of lucidity, he did mention what were supposedly Kitty's last words on earth: "Why are you doing this? Tell me why."

No one will ever know.

# 2

# THE MOON MURDERER

*"I'm not ashamed to admit that I viewed
her body through a mist of tears."*
*Detective Chief Inspector Jack Capstick.*

Staff Nurse Gwen Humphreys was standing by the
hospital windows, watching the full moon riding in a
cloudless sky. She had always loved the moonlight and
never ceased to be amazed by its ability to transform a
drab world. Tonight the moon had touched the grounds
of Blackburn's Queen's Park Hospital with magic.

It was one o'clock in the morning of Saturday, May 15,
1948, and Gwen was on a leisurely tour of the wards. She
always left Ward CH3 to the last, because this was the
"tiny tots" ward, and the one she enjoyed the most. Even
the most mischievous of children have a touching air of
innocence when asleep.

Coming into the ward, she felt a breeze and saw that
the porch doors were open. The door catches were known
to be faulty, so there was no immediate cause for alarm.
She closed them and began to check the cots. At cot
number four, her heart missed a beat. There was just an
empty mattress where three-year-old June Anne Devaney
should have been sleeping. The pillow was still warm to
the touch.

Gwen noticed three things. Firstly, the cot's drop sides

were still in place. Even the lively June Devaney couldn't have climbed over those. The child must have been lifted out. Secondly, there was a large Winchester storage bottle beneath the cot that hadn't been there before. It had been taken from an instrument trolley at the far end of the ward. And thirdly, there were muddy footprints on the highly-waxed floor leading from the porch door to the side of the cot. . . and back again.

It didn't require a Sherlock Holmes to deduce that someone had carried June Devaney through that door and out into the night. Gwen and the ward sister searched the immediate area in vain and then called in the police. The battered body of the little girl was soon found by a constable in the shadows close to the boundary wall. She had suffered terrible head injuries and there were signs of sexual interference.

Blackburn's chief constable, Mr. Looms, was roused immediately to find himself faced with a difficult decision. Should he allow his own officers to handle the case or risk their displeasure by calling in Scotland Yard's Murder Squad? This was a constant dilemma for chief constables in the immediate post-war years. Many of the provincial police officers resented the growing reputation of Scotland Yard. They felt that their own local knowledge, particularly their knowledge of local villains, more than counter-balanced the wider experience and superior forensic methods of the Yard. But on this occasion, Mr. Looms was wise enough to anticipate the town's anger at this brutal murder of a child and the pressures that would mount against the police, unless this case was solved very rapidly.

So after a brief conference with his senior officers, he put through a call to London; and at four o'clock in the morning, the dreams of Detective Chief Inspector Jack Capstick were interrupted by the ringing of the phone beside his bed.

He listened in silence and then, a man of few words, simply said, "Okay, I'm on my way." He added as an afterthought, "I'll need Flapper." Detective Inspector Wilf

'Flapper' Daws (so known because of his large ears) had for long been Capstick's righthand man.

Blackburn was about to receive the man who would become perhaps the most legendary of all the Scotland Yard commanders. Jack Capstick had first made his name at Bow Street in the early twenties. Bow Street was then the elite London force and it was surprising that Capstick had been accepted; because although burly and tough, he was below the regulation height. . . and Bow Street prided itself upon the size of its officers. Still a chief inspector from the north had described him as "the best thief catcher I've ever known," and this doubtless helped. But his start at Bow Street was scarcely auspicious. On his first night on patrol in the tough Seven Dials area, he was lured into an alleyway by three of the local tearaways and beaten up. He came staggering back into the station, his face covered in blood.

Hector Todd, a man mountain, was the desk sergeant that night and he viewed his latest recruit with scant sympathy. "You won't be much use to me, lad," he said, "if you fall for a mug's trick like that. I haven't the time to be a nursemaid."

But Capstick wasn't seeking sympathy. "I'll be looking out for them," he vowed, "and next time we meet, they'll be the ones who need the nursemaids. I'll make sure of that."

Hector Todd nodded slowly. "Maybe you will at that," he said.

Three weeks later, Capstick was passing the Coach and Horses public house in the Strand when a disturbance broke out inside and men began to leave rather hurriedly. He was told that some hooligans were breaking up the bar. He went inside and spotted his three friends from the alley busily engaged in smashing bottles and putting the fear of God into the staff.

Capstick addressed the shaken landlord. "Leave these three to me," he said, drawing his truncheon. "Get everyone else outside and bolt the doors."

A crowd gathered on the pavement outside, listening to the sounds of battle from within and fearful that they were about to witness the demise of a police officer. After ten minutes, the doors were opened from within and three tearaways emerged, bathed in blood. Capstick, seemingly unscathed and cool as the proverbial iceberg, followed them the truncheon still in his hand. "All right," he said quite casually, "we'll walk to Bow Street and the first one to get any other ideas can expect a tap from me."

And with that, he marched the three of them along a crowded Strand to Bow Street. It was his way of informing the criminal fraternity that he'd arrived; and that from now on, they had a new hunter on their patch. Following that day's work, he became known as 'Johnny Wood' and in any roughhouse, his truncheon would become a fearsome weapon.

Senior officers in those days came almost exclusively from the Hendon Police College. But Capstick broke the mould by rising from the ranks. There was just no stopping the man. His arrest record put him pretty much in a class of his own. Even on his days off, he would go looking for villains. He appeared to have an uncanny sixth-sense; and he claimed that when interviewing a suspect, he would know within thirty seconds whether the man was lying or telling the truth. . . and his record suggests that this was no mean boast.

His methods wouldn't have been tolerated in any modern force; for in a bid to obtain constant information, he mingled freely with the underworld. It was his boast that whenever a major gangland crime was committed, he would know the names of the men involved within the hour. Many of the top villains of the day regarded him with respect. Darby Sabini, the Italian who commanded the most powerful gang Britain has known, described him as "the gamest copper I ever knew." By way of explanation, he added, "on any raid led by Johnny Wood, he'd be the first man through the door, that big club swinging in his hand. He loved a roughhouse. He could hand it out and he could take it too."

Capstick had his own code. On many occasions after he'd supplied the evidence that sent a man to prison, he'd look after his family while he was inside and have a job waiting for him when he came out. His own men idolised him, but that admiration wasn't always shared by senior officers, many of whom were just longing for the day when he'd fall flat on his face. This was due partly to jealousy, partly to the fact that he was no respecter of rank. Given the choice, he would much rather have a drink with the village bobby than the chief constable. He was still a beat bobby at heart.

Upon arrival in Blackburn, he went straight to the hospital and years later, he described the scene that met his eyes by saying, "I'm not ashamed to admit that I viewed her body through a mist of tears. Detective service had hardened me to many terrible things; but this tiny pathetic body with its nightdress soaked in blood was something no man could see unmoved, it haunts me to this day."

The head of the Lancashire Fingerprint Bureau, Chief Inspector Colin Campbell, had already collected a large number of fingerprints from the ward, including some from the Winchester bottle. Eventually all the prints on the bottle were accounted for. . . except for one. There were no matching prints on file; but Capstick was convinced that this was the fingerprint of the killer of June Devaney.

It was a difficult case, because there was no apparent motive and seemingly no link between the murderer and his victim. From the very beginning, Capstick was worried about the implications of the full moon. He feared that he was dealing with a psychotic killer who would be driven to kill again and again. All known sex offenders in the area were interviewed and their alibis checked. An appeal to the public brought in a host of calls. . . reports of neighbours who had been acting strangely. . . sightings of men slinking through the shadows on the night of the murder. . . and numerous theories. All were investigated and found wanting. And as the weeks went by without an arrest, the public pressure mounted.

Capstick avoided the temptation of saying that an arrest was imminent. He was also too honest to say that the police had discovered vital clues which would eventually lead them to the killer.

Capstick was left with three beliefs, which he admitted were little more than hunches.

1. He believed that the unmatched print upon the bottle belonged to the murderer.

2. He believed that it belonged to a local man; because no stranger would have known the hospital grounds so well. The actual murder had been carried out in the most secluded patch of all.

3. He believed that this was a moon murderer, a man who would be driven to kill and kill again.

It was this final hunch that persuaded Capstick to take the greatest gamble of his career. Despite his rough, tough ways, he was a sentimental man at heart and exceptionally fond of small children; and he couldn't bear the thought of another tiny mite suffering the same fate as June Devaney. So against the advice of senior officers, he decided to take the drastic step of fingerprinting every male over the age of sixteen who had been in Blackburn on either the 14th or 15th of May.

There was a public outcry. City councillors and civil liberty organisations insisted that the idea should be abandoned. Some demanded that Capstick should be replaced; but the man himself stood firm. "We are talking about the safety of small children," he said. "With this at stake, what kind of man would refuse to cooperate?" That argument won the day, but he had no illusions. If this plan failed to unearth the killer, his own high-flying career would lie in ruins. The internal politics of Scotland Yard would see to that.

The mammoth task of fingerprinting an entire town was undertaken by a team of twenty officers led by

Inspector Bill Barton. To placate the natives, the Chief Constable promised that all the prints would be destroyed just as soon as the investigations were complete. The job took two months and none of the 46,000 prints taken matched the one on the bottle. Capstick's enemies were secretly delighted.

He slept fitfully that night, still stubbornly convinced that his original hunch had been right. And then just before the dawn, a thought came to him. The names for the fingerprinting had been taken from the electoral register. But there was one group of men whose names wouldn't appear on the register. . . those who had recently been released from the Services. He dressed immediately and arrived at the nearby police station in the half-light of day and phoned Scotland Yard, setting the wheels in motion. By noon, he had a new batch of names to be checked; and by nightfall, he had tasted success. Fingerprint No. 46253 matched the one found on the Winchester bottle. The print belonged to 22-year-old Peter Griffiths of 31, Birley Street, Blackburn, a man who had been released from the Army only a few months earlier.

Capstick decided to make the arrest personally. So early the following morning as Griffiths left home for work at a local flour mill, he was confronted by the burly figure of the detective known as Johnny Wood. There were no dramatics. Capstick cautioned him quietly and they were driven to the police station in the back of an unmarked car.

They barely spoke during the journey; but Capstick took the opportunity to study his prisoner along the way. He had been expecting a monster, but had found instead a clean-cut young man. . . on the surface at least, the kind of young man most parents would have been proud to have as their son. He had the upright bearing of a soldier and clear, untroubled eyes.

At the station, Capstick took him to the interview room and began to question him formally. At first, Griffiths denied everything. He said he couldn't remember where he'd been on the night of the murder. It was too long ago and he was quite incapable of committing any crime of violence against a child. But Capstick noticed that his hands had begun to open and shut, giving some hint of the turmoil within. So he said almost kindly, "Sonny, don't you think you'd feel a whole lot better if you told me what really happened that night?"

Griffiths let the silence drag out and then suddenly said, "You're right, of course, I killed her and the memory of that night has haunted me ever since."

He then made the following statement:

"I want to say that on the night the little girl was killed at the Queen's Park Hospital, it was a Friday night, the Friday before Whitsun. I left home that night on my own about six o'clock. I went to spend a quiet night on my own. I went to the Dun Horse pub and bought myself about five pints of bitter beer. Then I went to Yates's Wine Lodge and had a glass of Guinness and two double rums. I then had another glass of Guinness and went back to the Dun Horse. I then had about six more pints of bitter.

"I was on my own and came out of there at closing time. I walked down Jubilee Street off Darwen Street and I saw a man smoking a cigarette and sitting in a small closed car with the hood on and wire wheels. They were painted silver. I did not know him. I had never seen him before. I asked the man for a light, as I had no matches to light my cigarette. I stayed gabbing to him for about fifteen minutes. He said to me, 'Are you going home?' I said, 'No, I'm going to walk around a bit first and sober up.' He asked me where I lived and I told him. He said, 'Well, get in, open the window and I'll give you a spin.'

"He took me to the front of the Queen's Park Hospital and I got out opposite the iron railings. I don't know what happened to him. I never saw him again. I must have got over the railings, for the next thing I remember was being outside the ward, there were some children. I left my shoes outside the door, which had a brass knob. I tried the door and it opened to my touch. I just went in and heard a nurse humming and banging as though she was washing something. So I came out and waited a few moments.

"I went back in again and went straight to the ward like. I think I went in one or two small rooms like a kitchen and then I went back into the ward again. I then picked up a biggish bottle off a shelf. I went halfway down the ward with it and then put it down on the floor. I then thought I heard the nurse coming. I turned round sharply, overbalanced and fell against a bed. I remember the child woke up and started to cry, and I hushed her. She then opened her eyes, saw me and the child in the next bed started whimpering.

"I picked the girl up out of the cot and took her outside by the same door. I carried her in my right arm and she put her arms around my neck and I walked with her down the hospital field. I put her down on the grass. She started crying again and I tried to stop her from crying, but she wouldn't do, like she wouldn't stop crying. I just lost my temper and don't know what happened then. I banged her head against the wall. I then went back to the verandah outside the ward, sat down and put my shoes on. I then went back to where the child was. I just glanced at her, but didn't go right up to her, but went straight down the field to the dell. I crossed over the path alongside the dell leading into Queen's Park. I walked through the park and came out on Audley Street. I went down Cherry Street into Furthergate. Then I went down Eanam to Birley Street and got home somewhere around two o'clock on Saturday morning. It would be somewhere about that time. I went into my house, took my collar and tie off and slept in my suit on the couch downstairs. Mother and father were in bed and did not know what time I came in. I woke up about nine o'clock, got up, washed and shaved, then pressed my suit because I was going out again after I had had my breakfast.

"I went out then down the town, had a walk around, then went to the Royal cinema in the afternoon, came out of the pictures at five o'clock, went home and had my tea. I looked at the papers and read about the murder. It didn't shake me, so I just carried on normally after that. My mother and father asked me where I had been that night and what time I came home. I told them I had been out boozing and had got home at twelve o'clock. This is all I can say and I'm sorry for both parents' sake and I hope I get what I deserve."

The confession appeared to be both complete and open, but Capstick wasn't entirely satisfied. He went to Griffiths' home, armed with a search warrant. In the bedroom, he found a diary. He turned the pages until he came to May 14 where Griffiths had scrawled, "The moon is full. It is calling for blood and so tonight I must kill." Those chilling words washed away the last remaining doubts from Capstick's mind. His instincts had served him well.

Griffiths' parents were understandably stunned. They just couldn't believe that the son they'd loved could have committed such a terrible crime. Capstick described them as "two of the most decent people you could ever hope to meet." He admitted that he felt almost as sorry for them as he did for the parents of June Devaney. Nor were Griffiths' parents alone in refusing to believe his guilt. His former Army commander, his foreman at the flour mill and his workmates all spoke up in his praise. According to them, he was hard-working, friendly and totally honest . . .the perfect citizen, no less.

His trial for murder began on October 15 before Mr. Justice Oliver; and although he pleaded not guilty, the prosecution built up an overwhelming case against him. Besides the confession and the fingerprint evidence, the police had taken scrapings from the imprints left in the wax on the ward floor. These revealed fibres which matched fibres from Griffiths' clothing and fibres taken from the nightclothes worn by the victim. Bloodstains were found on Griffiths' trousers and jacket. The blood group was A, the same type as that of June Devaney.

The jury retired and twenty-three minutes later returned a verdict of guilty. Wearing the black cap, Mr. Justice Oliver said, "Peter Griffiths, this jury has found you guilty of a crime of the most brutal ferocity. I entirely agree with their verdict. The sentence of the court upon you is that you be taken from this place to a lawful prison and thence to a place of execution and that you there suffer death by hanging and that your body be afterwards buried within the precincts of the prison in which you shall have been confined before your execution. And may the Lord have mercy on your soul."

Griffiths nodded as though to indicate that he understood, but showed no sign of emotion. He then turned and walked smartly to the cells below.

On November 19, he was hanged by perhaps the most famous of all executioners, Albert Pierrepoint. And later when asked about Griffiths, Pierrepoint replied simply, "He died like a soldier."

And so two sets of parents were left to grieve for their loved ones. Jack Capstick returned to Scotland Yard where he would in turn command the Ghost Squad, Flying Squad and Murder Squad, a unique trinity. And back in Blackburn, Staff Nurse Gwen Humphreys had lost her love for the moonlight.

# 3

# THE SAXTON GRANGE AFFAIR

*"Ought to burn" or "Otterburn".*
*Ernest Brown's mysterious final words,*
*overheard by hangman Tom Pierrepoint.*

Dolly Masters, the village belle of Towton, lay sated across a crumpled double bed. Her silky black hair was spread out across the white pillow, her eyes were filled with dreams, her lips curved in a secret smile. She had the look of a very satisfied lady. Ernest Brown was propped on one elbow, studying her.

With her wickedly long legs, Dolly was the inevitable principal boy in every village pantomime, very young and very lovely; and that was the way he liked them. He traced a line across her ribs with a delicate fingertip and smiled as she wriggled beneath his touch. He circled her right breast, apple-shaped and firm as only the young can be; and then very, very gently he began to stroke the pink nipple and his smile became broader as it responded instantly.

"Can't you ever have enough?" he asked.

"Not of you," she said, and the reply pleased him.

He played the sex game the way he rode horses . . . with a cold heart and magic hands. He liked to feel that every woman he slept with had never had a lover quite so good before and would never know one quite so good again. Very few of that already long line of lovers would have quarrelled with the claim.

For here was a man who seemed to have everything. He was as handsome as any movie star, wild in his ways and quite fearless. To the maidens and the matrons alike of this North Yorkshire village, he could have been a visitor from another planet. They had never seen anything quite like him before. Their own menfolk, hardworking, dour and honest, appeared suddenly uninteresting when ranged alongside this swashbuckler of a man. There was barely a woman in the village who hadn't secretly dreamed of having an affair with Ernest Brown; and knowing this, he plundered them as the fancy took him.

. Normally in this part of Yorkshire, anyone who bedded another man's wife did so with extreme caution, fearful of discovery. But Brown wasn't like that at all. He appeared to flaunt his conquests of married women, as though daring the husband to do something about it. He boasted openly, "No woman who ever sleeps with me will ever be able to obtain total satisfaction with another man." It was a claim oft repeated by the women of Towton, and one that did his cause no harm at all.

But it was because of this quote that Dolly Masters had decided not to sleep with him. The decision had little or nothing to do with ethics. She longed to be an actress, to move from Yorkshire to the magic theatreland of London; and she believed that Ernest Brown was maybe the kind of man who could make such dreams come true. Only she would need to play him along a little, make him realise that she wasn't such an easy touch as the girls who had gone before. She would obviously let him kiss her good-night on the first date; but he would have to wait, show her respect, before they became lovers.

At least that had been the plan; but Brown had surprised her. He had taken her to a movie, followed by a meal and been the perfect gentleman. No sly innuendoes, no talk of sex. Instead he had listened to her hopes and dreams and shown a real interest; saying that he would like to help if he could, but making no rash promises. So when he had invited her back to his room for a late-night coffee, it had seemed churlish to refuse. And finally when he kissed her, the kiss was gentle, even tender, and because she was essentially a romantic, she found herself responding rather more warmly than she would have wished. He began to stroke her bare shoulders and neck; and she made no move to stop him, for she didn't wish to be considered a prude. His fingers continued to trace their patterns, the kisses gradually became more passionate; and the sensation was so tantalising, so delicious that she just didn't want it to stop. And then before she fully realised what was happening, he'd unhooked her bra and his hands were slipping inside her dress with practised ease.

She even opened her mouth to make the well-rehearsed claim "I'm not that sort of a girl," but her tongue refused to obey the message from her brain. Her body was turning traitor, betraying her with every passing second. And by then, of course, it was already too late. When he finally carried her naked to bed, she was in a transport of joy. No young bride ever went more willingly to her wedding bed.

His technique seldom varied. Slowly and surely, never hurrying, he would take a girl to the brink, then retreat a little, repeating the process over and over again. Sometimes for half an hour at a time he would keep her in a state of suspended ecstasy. And then in his own good time he would take them, bringing them to a climax so shattering that the ceiling would spin before their eyes.

Now filled with the foolish fantasies of the young, she had convinced herself that this was true love; and the experience gave her a feeling of confidence.

"Was it ever that good before?" she asked.

He smiled, recognising the motive behind the question. "Not bad," he said, "not bad at all. But then with me, it's always good."

She responded to his mood. "You mean you never fail to please?"

"Never," he said instantly.

She couldn't resist the temptation. "Well, tell me," she said, "if it's always so wonderful why did Mrs. Morton send you packing?" It was common knowledge in the village that he'd had a year-long affair with Dorothy Louise Morton, the young wife of his employer, Frederick Morton, a cattle-breeder of Saxton Grange Farm. And that she had finally chosen to end the affair.

Dolly had been unprepared for the sudden transformation. All the boyish charm went away. His eyes turned cold and angry.

"That silly bitch chose to go back to that fool of a husband when she could have had everything, me and the world on a plate. But don't worry, she'll come crawling back if I ever want her again. They always do."

Half an hour later, he was once more engaged in his sexual brinkmanship and Dolly was writhing around like a wild thing. But she had unwittingly seen the darker side of Ernest Brown, something she would have good cause to remember in the months ahead.

For underneath that aura of charm that Brown wore and discarded at will, there was a violent and dangerous man. At the age of eleven, he'd been birched for theft; and during his days in the Army, he'd been constantly dumped in the cells for desertion and assault. Around the Yorkshire pubs, he had built up a fearful reputation as a bar-room brawler. He was said to have fast hands and a hair-trigger temper. But for most of the time, he was still seemingly capable of pouring on the charm whenever he wished.

It was during the summer of 1933 that the darker side of his nature took over. It began with a disagreement with his boss, Frederick Morton, over the precise extent of his duties. In the middle of the discussion, Brown stormed off, shouting, "You can keep your lousy job." A few days later, he returned and asked to be reinstated. Morton agreed to take him back, but only as an odd-job man.

Thus the seeds of tragedy were sown. Apart from an ability to charm women out of their little cotton socks,

Brown's only true talent lay with horses. He could ride and groom them with a magic touch. Now the horses had been taken away from him and instead he'd been given a lowly position on the farm which dented his pride. He blamed Morton for all his current misfortunes. Morton had taken away his job and Morton had taken away his woman. Illogical thinking, of course; but there can be little doubt that Brown had looked upon the youthful Dorothy Morton as his passport to fame and fortune. In addition to her beauty, she also had the wealth for which he hungered.

In the days that followed, he became increasingly bitter and aggressive. On at least two occasions, he threatened to wreck the farm; and was clearly spoiling for a fight with just about anyone. The other farm workers stayed out of his path. Eventually the farm bailiff, James Stewart, went to Morton, saying, "Look here, this man is dangerous. He must be dismissed." But Morton declined to do so. . . an odd decision when you consider that he must have known Brown had been sleeping with his wife.

For Dorothy Morton, this was a time of torment. Like so many other young women, she had allowed herself to be seduced by this practised charmer; and now she regretted her weakness. She feared him too, being too well aware of the violence in his being. Her husband frequently went away on business, often staying overnight in some distant hotel. These were the times she feared the most, knowing that Brown still wanted her and that he was quite capable of rape if that would serve his ends.

On such occasions, she leant heavily upon the protection of Miss Anne Houseman, her two-year-old daughter's nurse. On September 5, 1933, this help would never be needed more.

Morton was away on yet another business trip and Brown was out drinking with friends, pouring on the charm in preparation for a little more plundering. At 8.15 p.m. he left his friends, promising his latest conquest that he would return shortly with one of Morton's two cars and drive her to Leeds.

At roughly the same time, Morton was drinking at the Boot and Shoe Inn near Garforth. After buying some cattle fodder, he set off for home around 8.45 p.m.

Back at Saxton Grange, Dorothy Morton was already trying to prevent Brown from taking one of her husband's cars, an Essex and a Chrysler. "Wait until Fred comes home," she urged. "You just can't go driving other people's cars without permission."

"What the hell's that got to do with you, woman?" shouted Brown, punching her in the face.

She turned and ran back into the house, followed by Brown who was looking very wild. Coming through the door, he hesitated for a moment when he saw Anne Houseman standing with her arm around Dorothy. Then he pushed past them, picked up a shotgun and went out again.

At half-past-nine, the two women heard a shot close to the kitchen window. Terrified, they hid under the dining-room table.

A little later, Brown returned to the house; and Anne Houseman asked him what he'd shot. "Only a rat," he said.

"In that case," she suggested, "give me the gun. You're beginning to scare everyone."

"Go to hell," he said, and once more stormed out of the house, still carrying the gun.

Both women would later testify that there was a wildness in Brown's face that bordered on madness. They listened desperately for the sound of Frederick Morton's car arriving. Then at half-past eleven, they heard wheels in the driveway, but no engine noise. Shortly afterwards Brown came into the house and said, "The boss has been in and gone out again."

They last saw Brown when he left the house around midnight. He still had that same mad look on his face; and that look so scared the two women that they went upstairs and locked themselves first in the bathroom, then later in Anne Houseman's bedroom.

Every now and then, they would hear the stairs creak. Someone was creeping around the house, searching for something or someone. They knew that this was almost certainly Brown searching for them.

At half past three in the morning, they heard a crackling sound followed by a dull explosion. Then looking out of the window, they saw the drive lit by a fire in the barn-cum-garage.

Miss Houseman ran to the telephone to call the fire brigade only to discover that the line was dead. Now desperate, Dorothy snatched her daughter from her cot and they ran across the fields to Towton, where they raised the alarm.

When the brigade arrived at Saxton Grange, the fire was burning fiercely. But they managed to fasten a rope to the four-door Chrysler and pull it out. Inside the burnt-out wreck was the charred body of Frederick Morton.

The police investigation was led by Detective Superintendent W. Blacker. A post-mortem revealed that one small piece of skin on Morton's abdomen had somehow survived the fire. It clearly showed a shotgun wound; and inside the body, they found twenty-eight shotgun pellets.

The two cars were examined and it was discovered that the draining plugs had been removed, allowing petrol to flow freely. Close to the cars, the police found a pair of pliers that belonged to Brown. The same pliers had been used to cut the telephone wires outside the house.

On the morning of September 7, Brown was arrested and charged with the murder of Frederick Morton. That afternoon, he was taken back to Saxton Grange to attend the inquest. Morton's body lay in an adjoining room throughout the proceedings.

The trial, which is regarded as a classic, was held before Mr. Justice Humphreys in December.

The prosecution, mainly through their forensic science experts, built up a strong case against Brown. They stated that he'd shot Morton at about 9 p.m., then fired a second shot, saying he was shooting at rats. He left the body in the car, then cut the telephone wires so that when the fire started, some time later, the brigade wouldn't arrive until after the body had been completely destroyed.

Spots of blood were found on Brown's boots and on a shotgun removed from the farm. The prosecution pointed out that Brown was fully dressed when the blaze broke out, and that his bed had not been slept in that night.

The defence suggested Morton had been murdered by another of Dorothy Morton's lovers. But the judge waived this aside during his summing up when he said, "The prosecution say there is proved evidence which shows that Brown committed the crime; because he must have been that man, for the evidence did not fit any human being but him."

The jury retired and, after an hour and twenty minutes, found Brown guilty. The judge, in passing sentence, said, "The jury have convicted you of a murder which was both cruel and brutal. I think it right to say I fully agree with their verdict."

Despite the callousness of the murder, ten thousand people signed a petition for mercy. The petition was sent to the Home Secretary, Sir John Gilmour, who postponed the execution under the Criminal Lunatics Act of 1884. This was to enable Brown to have further mental examinations.

The doctors could find no reason to interfere with the sentence, and Brown was duly executed on the morning of February 6, 1934.

Murders involving fires designed to destroy the victim's body are comparatively rare; and yet there had been another such murder three years earlier just down the road, so to speak, at Otterburn.

Late in the evening of January 6, 1931, a bus driver spotted a blazing car on the Newcastle to Otterburn Road. He stopped to investigate, and was shocked to discover that the car was a taxi belonging to his employer. Near to the cab lay his boss's daughter, Evelyn Foster. . . severely burnt, but still alive.

Although in great pain, Miss Foster was able to give a very lucid account of the events leading up to the fire. She said that she had picked up a fare in Otterburn who'd asked to be taken to Ponteland. During the journey, the man had changed his mind and ordered her to turn back to Otterburn.

When she'd asked him why, he became furious. He assaulted her, poured petrol over both the taxi and herself, then set fire to them.

She remembered the wild look in his eyes, the sense of being in the presence of a madman. But up to that outbreak of violence, he had apparently been charming. The description she gave would have fitted Ernest Brown quite neatly. But sadly she was never able to make a positive identification; because she died from her injuries the following day.

The police discounted her story. They suggested instead that she had accidentally set herself alight while burning the car for insurance purposes. They were satisfied, so they said, that the man she'd described didn't exist.

Her family were understandably outraged; because in effect, this suggested that their daughter had died while committing a criminal act. But try as they might, they were powerless to take the matter further.

The affair would have ended there if Ernest Brown had stayed silent on the scaffold.

But just before Tom Pierrepoint released the trap, that dangerously handsome man was heard to mutter, "Out to burn" or "Otterburn". Pierrepoint was never quite sure which, but he suspected that the words might have been a confession.

# 4

# AN ORIENTAL HONEYMOON

*"Be sure to do it on the ship."*
*"Don't do it on the ship."*
*"Again consider on arrival in Europe."*
*The unexplained doodlings of Chung Yi Miao*
*which, according to the prosecution, referred to*
*the planned murder of his wife.*

Miss Crossley had a newspaper spread across her lap, but she wasn't reading it. Instead she was secretly studying the two honeymooners at the far end of the lounge; and there was something very close to envy in her eyes.

The Borrowdale Gates Hotel, situated at the southern end of Derwentwater in the Lake District, is a romantic spot. With its sweeping views of green hills and clear blue water, it had become a mecca for lovers the world over. But she doubted whether it had ever seen a more romantic-looking couple than this.

Wai Sheung Siu and her newly-wed husband Chung Yi Miao could have stepped straight out of the pages of a Phillips Oppenheim novel. Wai, a diminutive beauty wearing a slit silk skirt and the jewels of the Orient. . . Chung, tall, strong and darkly handsome.

Miss Crossley had been so fascinated by their appearance that she'd made a point of befriending them. Wai, so she learnt, was the daughter of a wealthy merchant from the island of Macao, just off the mainland part of

Hong Kong. On his death, she inherited his considerable fortune. She had been educated in the United States, where she completed her studies at Boston University in 1922 and returned to Hong Kong. In 1927, she had taken a collection of Chinese jade and other Oriental objets d'art to be sold in New York. It was there, in October, that she had met and fallen in love with her future husband.

Chung, aged twenty-eight, was, by his own account, a wealthy Chinese lawyer who had gone to America to further his education. They had been married in New York in May, 1928 and then set off on honeymoon. But not for them the hurried weekend in Brighton or anywhere else. For them, it was to be the grand affair. They started with a tour of America, enjoying the Florida sunshine, the Rockies, Niagara and Broadway. This was followed by a leisurely ocean cruise as they headed for England and Scotland, countries which neither of them had visited before.

In her imagination, Miss Crossley could picture Chung sweeping Wai up into his strong arms and carrying her off masterfully to the bridal chamber and a night of passion Valentino style. So far no one had ever swept Miss Crossley off to a bridal bed (or for that matter, any other kind of bed), but she lived in hope.

For a brief moment, she pictured herself being borne away by those same strong arms; and then unexpectedly a chill hand touched her heart. Despite the romantic image he created, there was something just a little bit frightening about Chung. She'd noted that one moment he would be smiling and then suddenly the smile would disappear as though it had never been there at all and in its place, the eyes would take on the look of a hunter. . . and then that look would go too and the smile would return.

At two o'clock in the afternoon of June 19, a Tuesday, the Oriental honeymooners set out for a walk. Despite the sunshine, there was a cool wind blowing across the lake and so Chung donned a light brown overcoat.

At four o'clock, he arrived back at the hotel alone, telling a maid in fluent English that his wife had found the weather cold and gone to the nearby town of Keswick to buy some warmer clothes.

Wai was still missing at dinner and Miss Crossley found Chung dining alone. "Are you quite sure your wife will be able to find her own way home?" she asked.

Chung shrugged. "Believe me," he said, "there's nothing to worry about. My wife is an experienced traveller. Normally I would have stayed with her; but I have a cold and she wanted me to return to the hotel and go to bed." He switched on his smile. "No one wants to have a cold on their honeymoon."

Miss Crossley pointed out that the buses from Keswick were few and far between. "The next one," she said, "is due at nine o'clock. Would you like me to meet it?"

The smile went away. "No, that won't be necessary," he said shortly. "She will not come by bus. She does not like the bus. She will hire a car."

His voice didn't carry any conviction and Miss Crossley had already sensed that something was terribly wrong. Just what could Wai be doing alone in Keswick, she asked herself, a town she'd never visited before and where the shops would have closed long ago.

It was ten o'clock before Chung showed any sign of anxiety. He asked a maid what he should do and whether she thought he ought to inform the police. She suggested that this would be the sensible thing to do; but he did nothing and went to bed.

While Chung had been calmly eating his evening meal, a farmer had spotted a woman lying beside a pool in a wood called Cumma Catta, situated about a mile from the hotel. He thought she was probably resting or sleeping. He didn't wish to approach her in such a lonely spot for fear of scaring her. But he had recognised her. She was, he said, "the Oriental woman staying in the hotel." He was telling this to a group of customers in a nearby pub when he was interrupted by an off-duty policeman, Detective Constable Pendelbury.

"She wouldn't be resting alone at this time of night," Pendelbury pointed out reasonably enough. "My guess is that she's either been taken ill or worse. I think we'd better go and take a look right now."

So saying, he placed his pint upon the bar untouched and left it there. He didn't mention it, but earlier that day he'd seen Chung walking away from that selfsame pool alone; and his detective's instincts were working overtime. They found Wai lying under an umbrella and Pendelbury needed just one look to know that she was dead. A white cord had been tied tightly around her slim throat and she had bled from the mouth. Her clothing had been pulled up and her underwear removed. She was still wearing her expensive diamond-studded watch, but her diamond solitaire ring and a platinum and diamond wedding ring were missing. So the outward signs at least suggested that Wai had been both raped and robbed.

Chung was summoned from his bed and told of the grim discovery. Only the use of the white cord was mentioned, but Chung immediately said, "It's terrible! My wife assaulted, robbed and murdered."

His brown overcoat was examined and found to be stained with blood. "The bloodstains were got in New York," he told the police.

A search of the hotel room was inconclusive. In Wai's jewel-case, there were several items of jewellery valued at around £3,500. There was no sign of the two missing rings she'd been wearing on the day of her death.

But later in one of Chung's suitcases, the police found two rolls of used camera film. A local photographer was asked to develop them; and as he unwrapped the second roll of film, the two missing rings fell out on the table.

Chung merely shrugged. "My wife," he said, "hid her belongings in peculiar places, so I'm not in the least surprised."

During the enquiries, the police were ably assisted by Miss Crossley who had become a veritable Miss Marple. She gave them the honeymooners' background and more importantly a very detailed account of Chung's behaviour and conversation during the day of the murder.

She also made one very intelligent observation, after the post-mortem had established the fact that Wai hadn't been raped. "Just who," she asked, "would wish to suggest rape and robbery as the motive for this murder? Surely only the husband. . . the one man on earth who would neither need to rape or rob his wife." That point was later taken up in much greater detail by the prosecution.

The trial took place before Mr. Justice Humphreys in Carlisle, England's most northerly assize court. And it was the piece of paper produced by the prosecution that created the sensation.

Upon that piece of paper, written in Chinese, were three sentences:

"Be sure to do it on the ship."

"Don't do it on the ship."

"Again consider on arrival in Europe."

Chung admitted that he'd written these sentences; but said that he couldn't remember why or what they referred to. The prosecution claimed that this had shown a clear intent by Chung to murder his wife, a plot hatched in the very early days of their honeymoon, or maybe even before the wedding vows had been exchanged.

But Chung had his own theory. "It was because my wife took such pride in her jewellery and made a great display of it," he said, "that she was robbed and killed."

He also said that he'd seen two Orientals following him first in Scotland and more recently in the Lake District. "These were the men who killed my wife," he cried, "not me." This defence was given some credence when other witnesses came forward to testify that they had also seen two Chinese men in Keswick on the day of the murder.

However the jury wasn't impressed. They found Chung guilty. Upon hearing the verdict, he attempted to make a speech attacking Mr. Justice Humphreys' handling of the trial. He was cut short by the judge who sentenced him to death, saying he fully agreed with the verdict.

Chung took his case to the Court of Appeal, where he dispensed with the services of his counsel. He was allowed to argue the case himself. In dismissing the appeal, Lord Chief Justice Hewart said the jury were abundantly entitled to find him guilty of "this truly diabolical and calculated murder."

He was hanged on December 6, 1928.

Many theories have been put forward as to the motive for this murder. One of the most popular is that Wai had undergone a gynaecological operation and that Chung feared she was sterile. Due to his fierce male pride, he killed her so that he would be free to remarry and produce a family. One flaw in this is that it would surely have been a lot simpler and a lot safer to obtain a divorce.

Miss Crossley's own theory, not to be discounted lightly, is more straightforward. She believed that Chung was simply in a hurry to inherit his wife's riches without any ties.

With her track record on the case, she may well have been right.

# 5

# THE GREEN LINNET

*"If any other verdict had been returned,
it would have been a bad day for
mothers-in-law." Lord Goddard, after
sentencing Alec Wilkinson to death.*

Mother-in-law jokes are always good for a laugh. So when
Alec Wilkinson ran down the road, shouting, "I've just
done my mother-in-law in," the worthy citizens of
Wombwell smiled broadly and waited for the punch line.

"I've polished off the old cow once and for all,"
announced Alec, leaping in the air and waving his arms
about in a very wild manner indeed. He was laughing and
the bystanders laughed with him. Then they saw the blood
on his hands and the laughter stopped.

These Yorkshire folk had good reason to be surprised.
For Alec Wilkinson a 22-year-old miner, was one of the
best-liked young men in the area with an amiable disposi-
tion. Later a visiting reporter would ask one of the older
miners to tell him what Alec was really like.

The old man paused, considering and then he said,
"Alec reminds me a little of the story about the funeral of
the man nobody liked. Afterwards a handful of mourners
stood around the grave, desperately trying to think of
something nice they could say about the deceased.

"Finally one of them spoke up. 'He was,' he said 'a very
good speller at school.' Now that you can be sure would

have been Alec. He always tries very hard to say something good about everyone."

But seemingly he found it virtually impossible to say something good about his mother-in-law, the 50-year-old Clara Farrell. . . a lady with a rather dubious reputation who had for long been known around the local pubs as 'The Green Linnet'.

He had married her young daughter Maureen eight months earlier and they'd lived for a time with his parents. But she had become unhappy with this arrangement and so returned to her own parents.

This was when the troubles began. Alec idolised his wife and missed her terribly. He blamed his mother-in-law for the breakdown of the marriage, and there were frequent rows.

On one occasion, he had taken a day off from work because he was feeling unwell. Mrs. Farrell had then subjected him to a tirade of abuse. . . claimed that while his wife was out working, he was at home 'laking' (playing). She told him he ought to go into the Army; and when he asked who would pay the hire-purchase instalments and keep Maureen, she supposedly stated that Maureen would have to become a prostitute.

In another quarrel, he told Mrs. Farrell that he knew all about her notoriety as 'The Green Linnet', to which she replied, "I was driven to it. The same as Maureen will be before tha' gets her back."

He made repeated attempts to persuade Maureen to return to him, but always Mrs. Farrell barred the way. And on April 30, 1955, his patience finally gave way. He spent the day 'on the ale' brooding in his misery and craving to be with his wife again. After closing time that night he went to a cafe in Barnsley and had a cup of coffee. As he paid his bill, he said, "You won't be seeing me next week."

A pretty waitress smiled. "Is that a threat or a promise?" she asked, never dreaming for a moment that he was serious.

He took a taxi to Maureen's home and remarked casually enough that he was "going to do somebody in." The driver, like the waitress, laughed. "That's it, lad," he said. "You do them in."

It was just after midnight. Looking through the window, Alec could see Mrs. Farrell sitting alone beside the fire. He guessed that she was waiting up for Maureen to come home, a long-established habit of hers. So he decided to wait too. A few minutes later, Maureen arrived with two friends who had come to see her safely to her door. As soon as she had gone in, Alec knocked. Mrs. Farrell opened the door to be confronted by an Alec Wilkinson she had never really seen before. His normal easy going ways had been shed like a cloak and he was suddenly a very dangerous man indeed.

She told him to go away and, by way of answer, he punched her, knocking her to the ground. He then banged her head repeatedly on the floor. Maureen ran to help her mother, but was knocked unconscious by a single punch.

A next-door neighbour, Mr. Butler, had heard the bangs and screams. So he went to the front door of the Farrells and, as he stepped through, he heard the back door close. He found Maureen still unconscious and her mother dead. Furniture had been piled up and set on fire; and standing just inside the doorway were Maureen's two friends who had also heard the screams and come running.

After his triumphal run down the road, Alec made no real attempt to escape. He gave himself up seemingly quite happily and that strange euphoria stayed with him during the drive to the station in the police car.

He continued to laugh and shout, telling Sergeant Gilbertson, "I got the bread knife and stuck her with it. I piled the furniture over her and just as I was about to set it alight, the wife ran at me and I jumped her. If she gets over it, she'll have a stiff neck for a week."

On arrival at the station, he made a voluntary

statement. In this, he said that after his wife returned to her parents, he had tried to get her back many times without success. So after some heavy drinking, he had decided to make one last effort to see her.

He went on: "As soon as the door opened, my mother-in-law used foul language when telling me to go. She rushed at me and pushed me against the wall. It was enough to make anybody want to do her in. I just struck at her and everything went red. I knocked her down and banged her head. I kicked her. I would have hit her with the poker if I could have got hold of it. I then tried to set fire to the place."

The trial took place on June 20 before the formidable Lord Chief Justice, Lord Goddard. Sir Godfrey Russell Vick led for the Crown and Alec Wilkinson was represented by Mr. John Parris.

Wilkinson made little attempt to defend himself in court. In answer to Sir Godfrey, he said he disliked Mrs. Farrell intensely. He couldn't remember using a knife or pushing her legs into the fire. Nor could he remember why he'd started the fire at the house.

Finally Sir Godfrey asked, "Are you sorry for what you did to your mother-in-law?"

Wilkinson shook his head emphatically, "No sir," he said. "I'm not."

Dr J.L. Walker, the medical officer at Leeds Prison, told the court that he had found Wilkinson alert, of above average intelligence, hard-working and respectful. His conversation was rational and his behaviour normal. The doctor found no grounds for believing he had suffered a schizophrenic disorder.

Sir Godfrey submitted that the evidence was abundantly clear. Wilkinson had caused Mrs. Farrell's death by "most ghastly and horrible wounds with a knife upon her body."

Mr. Parris, addressing the jury, said that the defence wasn't asking for an acquittal. But he pointed out to them that if they felt that the prisoner had been severely provoked, this could have the effect of reducing the crime from murder to manslaughter.

However the jury found Wilkinson guilty of murder and Lord Goddard sentenced him to death. . . adding dryly that "if any other verdict had been returned, it would have been a bad day for mother-in-laws."

At the Court of Criminal Appeal, Mr. Parris argued that Lord Goddard had misdirected the jury on the issue of insanity, and had not put certain points of the evidence correctly.

But Lord Justice Hilbery replied, "The evidence does not come within miles of the McNaghten rules. In law, there was no case to go to the jury on the question of insanity. There was no other verdict possible but murder, and that was the verdict the jury most properly found. The appeal is dismissed."

Over 35,000 people signed petitions for Alec Wilkinson's reprieve, and testimonials flooded in. The manager at the colliery where he'd worked said, "I just can't speak too highly of him. He was hard working, honest, friendly and a thoroughly decent man." And many testified to his good nature and polite ways.

But words couldn't save him. He was hanged on August 12, 1955. He remained polite right to the very end. In his last letter, to be opened after his death, he wrote: "I should just like to add my grateful thanks to all the prison personnel with whom I came in contact while I was here in Leeds, from the Governor down to the prison officers. I can honestly say I received every consideration and assistance I could possibly have hoped for."

So died a young man who had allowed his own hatred for the only enemy he'd ever known to destroy him.

For a time at least in Wombwell, mother-in-law jokes would fall on stony ground. Everyone had stopped laughing.

# 6

# MISS UNTOUCHABLE

*"I am innocent and if the dead girl's
lips could only speak, they would tell you
the same." Alfred Bostock.*

It was the lunch break at the Parkgate Ironworks and as
Elizabeth Sherratt walked across the yard, the eyes of the
entire workforce followed her hungrily. She had a body
designed to torment men and the face of an angel, a deva-
stating combination on a hot summer's day.

An apprentice, bolder than the rest, whistled shrilly in
appreciation. She didn't miss a beat. Her stride remained
unchecked and nothing showed on that beautiful face.
One of the older men turned to the whistler. "You're
wasting your time, lad," he said. "That's Miss Untouchable. She's not interested in the likes of you and I."

And so it seemed. There was barely an able-bodied
man at the works who hadn't tried to chat her up at one
time or another. They'd invited her out for lunchtime
drinks, for evening meals, to dances and to the local
cinema in Rawmarsh on the outskirts of Rotherham. She
had thanked them pleasantly enough for their offers; but
always the answer had been "No".

So behind her back, they called her 'Miss Untouchable',
'Miss Iceberg' and 'Miss No Thanks'. And to protect their
male pride, they convinced themselves that this was simply

a prim maiden with no interest at all in the joys of sex.

They couldn't have been more wrong. On her first day at work, she had spotted a crane driver Alfred Bostock stripped to the waist, heavily tanned and built like an Adonis, muscles rippling. She had been fascinated by the sight. Bostock had taken one look at the new girl and been equally fascinated. So began a torrid love affair. It was the meeting of two bodies beautiful. But it had to be conducted in secret; for Bostock was already married. He told Elizabeth that the marriage was unhappy and that he was seeking a divorce, so that the two of them would be free to live together openly for ever. Still these are, after all, the words that cheating husbands have been using down the ages. . . and, like so many of the others who had gone before, Bostock didn't really mean them.

The very presence of Bostock at the ironworks ensured that Elizabeth continued to ignore all the advances that came her way. So she led a strange double life. Miss Prim by day, Miss Passionate by night. Certainly her workmates would have been astonished if they could have seen her in the latter role. The powerful Bostock was already confiding to friends that he was finding it difficult to keep up with the sexual demands of his latest lover. . . according to him, an insatiable lady.

In a bid to make their secret more secure, Elizabeth left the ironworks and took a job as an attendant at the Parkgate Electra Picture Palace. When Bostock came visiting, she would show him to a seat in the back row of the circle; and then once the film had started, she would snuggle up to him in the darkness.

One night, she had some very special tidings to impart. "Darling," she said, "I'm pregnant. We're going to have a baby." It was maybe fortunate that she couldn't see his face in the darkness. For this was the news he'd been dreading. And although she had no means of knowing, she had just signed her own death warrant. Bostock had no desire at all to see his marriage broken; and certainly no intention of being the party sued in a messy divorce case.

On May 3, 1925 Elizabeth Sherratt was found floating in the river at Rawmarsh. Her head had been savagely beaten. The police formed the opinion that she had fought her assailant hard, because splats of blood were discovered on bushes and on the towpath over a wide area.

Witnesses came forward to say that they'd seen her earlier that evening in the company of a good-looking and powerfully-built man. The description fitted Bostock. When the police made inquiries at the ironworks, one of Bostock's workmates said that a few weeks earlier the crane driver had mentioned that he was having trouble with a woman.

Then a search of Elizabeth's bedroom unearthed love letters written by Bostock. He was arrested and charged with wilful murder. The trial, which was described as being of a sensational nature, opened before Mr. Justice Finlay.

A doctor told the jury that Elizabeth's skull had been fractured in four places, and that she'd been dead before being thrown into the river.

Bostock's workmate told the court that in February the accused had told him that he was having a bit of bother with a woman and that he would have to get out of it in some way. The witness added that on the day before the murder, Bostock had said to him, "If I don't do her in before the weekend, my name's not Bostock."

In the witness-box, Bostock admitted that he had been Elizabeth's lover, but denied the statement that he'd intended to "do her in." He also admitted being with her on the night of the murder. . . but only, he said, for ten minutes. He'd spent the rest of the evening from eight to ten in the Forge and Rail Mill public house. This was rebutted by other customers who had been in the pub during the stated period.

One of them said, "Alfred Bostock wasn't the kind of man you'd miss easily. If he had been there, I'd have known."

Bostock's wife Ethel, quiet and pleasantly-spoken, said

that she'd walked home with her husband from her mother's house soon after ten o'clock on the night of the murder. Her husband had seemed quite normal and she'd had no reason to suspect that anything untoward had happened.

Mr. G.H.B. Streatfield, for Bostock, told the jury that all the evidence was circumstantial. He suggested that the fact that Bostock had spoken of his intention to "do the girl in" was in his favour. For no man intending to commit murder would speak of his intentions in such an open way.

Mr. G.F.L. Mortimer, for the Crown, made great play of the fact that the defence had found it impossible to find anyone who could support Bostock's claim that he'd spent most of the night of May 3 in the Forge and Rail Mill public house. "Why would an innocent man," he asked, "put forward a false alibi?"

The jury, which included three women, seemingly had no doubts. They deliberated for just fifteen minutes before bringing in a verdict of guilty.

When the clerk of the court asked Bostock whether he had anything he wished to say, he replied, "I am innocent and if the dead girl's lips could only speak, they would tell you the same."

Alfred Bostock was executed on September 3, together with Wilfred Fowler who had been convicted, with his brother, of the 'Sheffield Gang Murder.'

Elizabeth's workmates at the Parkgate Ironworks sent a large and imposing wreath to her funeral, its message simple and touching:

"To Elizabeth. . . from all the friends you never knew."

# 7

# A FAMILY AFFAIR

*"Why have you shot me, Charles?*
*I've done you no wrong."*
John Kew's words after being shot by
Charles Backhouse.

Nobody likes a cop, at least not all of the time. Mind you,
they have their uses. When we wake in the night and hear
footsteps in the lounge below, we won't hesitate. We'll lift
the bedside phone, dial 999 and be grateful when the boys
in blue arrive to do a job that we're not over anxious to
tackle ourselves. When injured after a car crash, we'll be
happy enough to have a comforting arm wrapped around
our shoulders and to be told, "Don't worry, you're going
to be all right. The ambulance is on its way." And when
the going gets really tough and they're dealing with
terrorists, armed bank robbers and the like, we'll even
cheer them on from a safe distance. But let these
guardians of the law put so much as a foot across our front
door and suddenly it's a very different matter. If they think
they can butt into our private lives, they're wrong and they
can butt right out again. . .

It was a bit like that in the mining village of Swinton at
the turn of the century. John Kew, the village bobby, was a
fine upstanding sort of chap, a good husband and a good
father to his four young children. He was even-tempered,

honest, kind and quite fearless. And as he pounded his daily beat, he picked up many an answering smile.

If only he hadn't made the mistake of butting into a family affair, it might have stayed that way. But when Fred Backhouse started to beat up his flirty-eyed sister-in-law Gertie Backhouse, John Kew elected to intervene. Seemingly he had an old-fashioned objection to women being bashed about. . . although it was well known in that day and age that the odd bit of thumping did wives a power of good. Apart from anything else, it made sure that the Sunday dinner arrived on the table at the right time.

However John Kew didn't see it that way. Not only did he stop Fred Backhouse before he'd had a chance to warm to his work, but he then charged him with assault. Fred was fined £2 with twelve shillings costs.

Gertie's husband Charles was initially upset to come home and find his wife sporting a shiner. This wasn't his brother's responsibility, he felt. If Gertie deserved a thumping, then he was the one who should have given it to her, and no one else. But the court case outraged him; and he was particularly angered by the fact that Gertie, during her spell in the witness box, had made no attempt to help Fred. On the contrary, she had happily buried him.

The Backhouse brothers became increasingly bitter with each passing day, and on the evening of July 10, 1900, they bought a six-chambered revolver from an ironmonger's shop at Parkgate, a few miles from their home in Swinton.

Later that night, they went to the High House Inn where they met three friends, John Wheeler, William Gibbins and Albert Thompson. The five men huddled in a corner of the pub, deep in conversation. Charles Backhouse said that no man could change his mind. Patting his pocket where the gun bulged, he added, "Death and glory, I shall not harm my wife."

Fred made a remark about John Kew and the fine he had to pay, then said, "Aye, we'll fettle that bugger."

At this last remark, Thompson became alarmed. He made his excuses, left and went straight to the police house where he spoke to Kew. He would explain later that his true purpose was an attempt to save the brothers from the consequences of their own foolishness.

"They've bought a gun and they're planning to shoot you tonight," he told Kew.

Kew shrugged. "That's just the ale talking, Albert," he said. "They're not the murdering kind. By tomorrow morning, they'll have slept it off and forgotten all about it."

Meanwhile Gibbins, Wheeler and the two brothers had left the pub and gone to Wheeler's house. Charles Backhouse was becoming more determined by the minute. He removed the revolver from his pocket and explained that it was six-chambered and fully loaded.

He then put his finger to his temple and said to Gibbins, "Not tonight, Bill, but in the morning. I shall not hurt my wife and child."

Wheeler's wife, Martha, watched Charles wave the gun about and was horrified. So she too slipped away to warn John Kew.

"Make no mistake," she said, "Charles means it. When he's in this kind of a mood there's no stopping him. Unless you can do something quick, he'll shoot you and then he'll shoot himself and perhaps poor Gertie too."

Kew put a reassuring hand on her shoulder. "Don't you worry, Martha," he said. "I'll go and talk to him man to man, and then he'll soon see reason."

But as Kew went through the garden gate of the Wheelers, the brothers emerged from the house.

Kew was calmness itself. "Charles," he said, "what's all this nonsense I hear about you planning to shoot me? Don't tell me that this fuss over a fine is worth dying for."

Charles was standing very still. "I don't know what you're talking about," he said.

Kew shook his head slowly. "Come on, Charles. You know I've got to search you, for your sake and mine. If you've got a gun, just give it to me and then we can forget that all this ever happened."

By way of answer, Charles took a pace backwards, drew the revolver and shot the policeman in the abdomen. Kew stumbled, but stayed on his feet. "Why have you shot me. Charles?" he asked, sounding more surprised than hurt. "I've done you no wrong."

Without a word, Charles passed the gun to his brother Fred, who shot Kew in the right hip, saying, "Here's another one for you, you bugger."

Despite his injuries, Kew grabbed hold of both brothers and dragged them to his police house, where they were held with the assistance of some men from the village.

Only then did the remarkable John Kew allow himself to be taken to hospital, where he died the following day. The hospital issued a statement, praising the courage and fortitude of the policeman. "We still find it incredible," said the statement, "that a man mortally wounded was still able to carry out an arrest of two strong men."

The brothers were jointly charged with murder and appeared before Mr. Justice Ridley on July 28. Mr. Thomas and Mr. Edmondson prosecuted; and Mr. Mitchell-Innes defended both prisoners.

During the course of his evidence, Gibbins said that when Charles Backhouse made the remark "Not tonight, Bill, but in the morning," he took this to mean that he was going to commit suicide.

The medical evidence was that death had been due to septic peritonitis, the result of the abdominal wound. Had the shot in the hip been the only one fired, the doctor's opinion was that Kew would have lived.

Police Inspector Danby said that when charged with murder, Fred Backhouse said, "Yes, we did it, but we were drunk at the time."

Charles simply said, "Yes."

Mr. Mitchell-Innes contended for the defence that as Fred Backhouse didn't fire the shot that caused death, he could only be regarded as a principal in the second degree. So the question was: "Did Charles commit murder?"

There was not one fragment of evidence, said Mr. Mitchell-Innes, to suggest that Charles bore the policeman any ill-will; and moreover it was apparent from his strange remarks and conduct that evening that he contemplated suicide.

It was Mr. Mitchell-Innes' hypothesis that it was Charles's strange and excited mood which had been responsible for what he described as "this tragedy."

Addressing the jury, he said, "I put it to you that when Kew attempted to search him, Charles drew the revolver from his pocket with every intention of handing it to his brother, and that it then discharged accidentally."

Mr. Justice Ridley (who was later described as a "curiously futile and undignified judge") summed up the case. He said that if two men went out together with a common design to use upon a person a weapon in such a way that death might result, and one of those persons fired a fatal shot, the second man would be equally guilty.

The question the jury had to decide was this: "Were the two brothers setting out that night with the sole purpose of using this weapon on the policeman, or had they obtained the gun for the totally different purpose of committing suicide as has been suggested?"

The jury retired and were absent from court for just over an hour. Upon their return, the foreman said they found Charles guilty of murder and Fred guilty of aiding and abetting.

The judge asked, "Do you mean he aided and abetted his brother during the crime, or that he consented after it was done? Do you mean that he was an accessory before the fact?"

The foremen replied, "That is the meaning of it, my Lord."

The judge paused. "I need to be quite sure about this," he said. "Are you saying that you think he was a party to it both before and at the time it was committed?"

"We do, my Lord."

"Have you any recommendations?"

"Yes, we recommend the prisoner Frederick Backhouse

to mercy because of his age."

The judge sighed. "For today that means a verdict of guilty against both prisoners."

Addressing the two prisoners, the judge said, "The jury have convicted you both of murder, and I think properly. The jury in your case, Frederick Backhouse, have recommended you to mercy. That will be forwarded to the proper quarter. It now only remains for me to pass upon you the sentence, the only sentence according to law."

The brothers heard the death sentence unmoved and left the dock without assistance.

Mr. Justice Ridley did forward the jury's recommend-ation to the proper quarter, which happened to be his brother Sir Matthew White Ridley, the then Home Secretary. A few days later, nineteen-year-old Frederick Backhouse was reprieved and his sentence commuted to penal servitude for life.

Charles Backhouse was not so fortunate. He was exe-cuted on August 16, 1900. James Billington was the hangman, assisted by his son William.

In the meantime, a strange thing had happened in the village of Swinton. John Kew had become a public hero. . . in fact something of a legend as the policeman who although mortally wounded was still courageous enough to arrest two dangerous men.

His funeral was attended by the entire village. And when they took a collection for his widow and four children, it was said that not a single man in Swinton failed to put his hand into his pocket.

By then, of course, Swinton (man, woman and child) had come to the conclusion that they rather liked John Kew. And much to their own surprise, they had begun to realise that, cop or no cop, they'd miss him.

# 8

# THE WORKING MAN'S FRIEND

*"I've done it! I'm not going to let a man like that
ruin your life." Thomas Richardson's
remark to his lover Laura.*

The Silver Slipper on the outskirts of Leeds was a pretty
sleazy sort of dump, filled with faded paint and faded
dreams. Indeed, just the sort of place where you would
expect to find a stripper known as Big Bertha high-
stepping her way along the bar.

Bertha knew all about faded dreams. She had once
dreamed about being a star of the silver screen, England's
answer to Mae West. For one heady year, she had been in
the chorus line at Drury Lane. But that was the nearest
she had ever come to fame. Ever since she had been on a
downward path. From London's West End, she had
moved to the seaside revues. She had stripped for a while
quite artistically in the Gipsy Rose Lee style, shielded
behind fans; but that career too had become a slippery
slide. The theatres had become increasingly rougher, the
act increasingly vulgar; and now at the Silver Slipper, she
had reached the end of the line. The once shapely thighs
had become heavy; and even the skilful use of paint and
powder upon her face could no longer disguise the
ravages of time.

Yet despite everything, she still enjoyed her hour upon

the stage where she was still a star of a kind. Tonight she was feeling surprisingly bright and bushy tailed, eager to strut her stuff. And much of this élan was due to the presence halfway down the bar of a raffish, jolly fellow known to just about everybody in the Silver Slipper simply as 'Doc.'

Oscar Wilde once remarked that "by the time a man gets to forty, he has the sort of face he deserves." If this was true, Doc was surely a very nice man indeed; for his face reflected an oceanic good nature. There were laughter lines around the eyes and the mouth was kind.

As Bertha came high-stepping her way down the bartop she asked, "How am I doing, Doc?"

"You're doing just fine," said Doc, "never better."

"Brother," she said, borrowing a line from Al Jolson, "you ain't seen nothing yet."

Everyone laughed and Doc laughed loudest of all; but it did seem as though tonight she was intent upon giving a very special performance. She had always been a stripper of the old school who believed in taking her time, building up the anticipation of her audience; but no one could remember her being quite so painstaking as this before. The buttons on her blouse were undone with tantalising slowness. The zipper on her skirt went up and down several times before that too was cast aside.

Now down to bra and panties (no spangles or G-string for Bertha), she was still in no hurry. She danced to the music, as though she had forgotten for a moment that stripping was her game. Yet she was all too well aware of the effect she was having on this rough and motley crowd. There were ever-mounting cries of "Get 'em off"; and tonight these were half-command, half-entreaty. She smiled, sensing the desire, her pleasure growing.

Finally, she knelt on the bar with her back turned to Doc and said, "Will you do the honours, Doc?"

Without a word, Doc unclipped her bra and slipped it down over her arms. The result was spectacular. Her mighty breasts sprang out as though on springs and incredibly there wasn't the slightest sign of sag. If anything, they were slightly upturned. Big Bertha had been well named after the giant siege gun of the First World War which had pounded the French defences from a distance of twenty miles. Bertha's matching pair were equally formidable. They may have owed something to a surgeon's nip and tuck; but tonight no one really cared.

As they were bared, there was an audible gasp in the Silver Slipper; and that sound was, for Bertha, the sweetest music. At this stage in her act, she knew that the audience would have stopped looking at her face. Even her thunder thighs would have taken on a certain appeal. But it was those remarkable breasts which would be commanding everyone's attention. She could sense the rising desire, even a certain admiration. . . and in these brief moments every night, her lost pride would return.

But on this occasion, it wasn't the mob's admiration that she hungered for. It was Doc's. To her, Doc represented style, the kind of style she liked to believe that she had once possessed during that brief sojourn at Drury Lane. He was an educated, sophisticated man and in this crowd, to Bertha at least, he stood out like a diamond in a cluster of glass.

Normally once her panties had been shed, Bertha's act would come to a rapid end; but not tonight. Instead she proceeded to high-kick her way along the bar, totally naked with everything bouncing and jouncing in the most delightful way. And then for a grand finale, she made a mock stumble and fell off the bar straight into the arms of Doc who caught her neatly.

Perched across his lap, she asked, "You going to stay and buy me a drink or two, Doc?"

Doc hesitated in something of a quandary. He had already made some elaborate plans to pay a surprise visit on a lonely young divorcee whom he was quite sure would welcome a little home comfort.

Bertha, aware of that hesitation, felt some of the elation

drain away. She had put herself out on a limb with no safety net. She had made an open pitch for Doc, and already sensed that he was about to say "No." To make matters worse, the club had gone quiet, as everyone waited to hear his answer.

To make matters a bit easier for him, she said hastily, "Maybe another night, Doc."

He was looking at her face and thinking that this was really a map of battles lost. He wondered too just how old she was; and he was anxious to choose his words carefully. Then he looked into her eyes and saw the pain.

Suddenly he smiled. "Luv," he said, "tonight you were a star and stars deserve to be wined and dined; so that's what we're going to do, you and I. Go and put your glad rags on and we'll paint the town red."

A few minutes later, they left the club arm in arm. A newcomer to the Silver Slipper watched them go, then turned to the bartender. "Who's that guy Doc?" he asked. "Is he a professional gambler or something?"

The bartender was amused. "You're thinking of Doc Holliday," he said. "No this one's a real-live doctor. . . Dr David Dewar to be precise. . . and a damn good one. He likes his ale and he likes his women; and some of the old biddies in the town complain about that from time to time. But you won't hear any beefs from around these parts. In our opinion, he puts most of the other doctors to shame."

It was a fair summing-up of this Scottish doctor who had become a legend in this area of Leeds during the Second World War. He was known as 'the working man's friend' and it was claimed that no call for help ever went unanswered. He would go out in the middle of the night, eternally cheerful; and if his patients were poor, he'd never charge.

But against this catalogue of good deeds, there was just one failing. He was a little careless in his choice of women and always liable to leap into bed with other men's wives. After six years of war, with many servicemen overseas, the opportunities for a man such as Doc were seemingly never-ending. For although in his early forties, he was still a considerable charmer. So there had always been the danger of him picking up the odd shiner from some miffed husband. Still, no one had expected to hear the news that spread like wildfire on Sunday, April 29, 1945.

At eight o'clock that morning, a workman had found Doc dead lying behind a car in the driveway of his own home. The ignition keys were still in his hand; and the police formed the opinion that he had been attacked from behind as he stooped to fasten the gates. There were at least ten wounds on the back of his head, and the skull had been shattered by a sharp-edged weapon.

The police, led by Detective Superintendent Jim Craig, checked all Doc's known haunts; and discovered that he had taken a married woman called Laura to a pub on the previous evening and remained there until 12.30 a.m. He had then driven her home, dropping her off about a quarter of an hour later and then returned to his own home.

Normally, in such cases, the husband would have been the first obvious suspect. But Laura's husband had the perfect alibi. He was a soldier serving in Italy.

The police painstakingly checked on Laura's private life and discovered that the Doc hadn't been her only clandestine lover. A 27-year-old engineer, Thomas Richardson, had also been visiting her by dead of night.

On May 21, Superintendent Jim Craig, accompanied by Inspector Thurkill, went to Richardson's house. As the engineer opened the door, he said, "I've been expecting you. I know you've got me well tied up."

He then made and signed a voluntary statement in which he admitted having killed the Doc. When asked about the murder weapon, he said he'd used an axe which he'd subsequently thrown into the River Aire. "I can remember seeing the splash when I threw it in," he said.

The trial opened on July 8 before Mr. Justice Hallett. The Crown was led by Mr. G.H.B. Stretfield and Richardson was represented by Mr. C.B. Fenwick.

One of the more unusual features of the trial were the number of women who crowded into the public gallery, many of whom had known Doc personally. They listened with considerable interest as Mr. Stretfield revealed what he termed "Dr Dewar's sleazy private world."

He said, "Dr Dewar's mode of life left a good deal to be desired. He was a good man of somewhat intemperate habits and associated with people of the lower-middle and lower classes, and of the greyhound fraternity. He was in the habit of frequenting public houses and clubs in the city of the less reputable type. He was unfortunately somewhat overfond of the opposite sex."

"Why unfortunately?" asked a female voice and laughter rippled through the gallery. The judge frowned and the laughter slowly died.

Counsel continued, "Among other women he associated with was the woman Laura, the wife of a soldier serving in Italy. The accused Richardson was also in love with Laura. He found out about Laura's association with the doctor and became very jealous."

When giving evidence, Laura told the court that on May 20, Richardson had told her, "I've done it. I'm not going to let a man like that ruin your life."

Superintendent Craig was asked by Mr. Fenwick about the axe. He admitted that despite every effort, they had failed to find it. The River Aire had been searched for two hundred yards on either side of the spot where Richardson said he'd thrown the murder weapon.

Richardson told the jury that he had never been in any trouble with the police. He said he'd become friendly with Laura about a year ago, and visited her mostly at night because he hadn't wanted their friendship to be known. He added that he was devoted to her and desperately jealous when she spoke to other men.

On the night of the murder, he said he'd arrived home at about 10.30 p.m. He had then woken at eight o'clock the following morning, feeling very ill.

He had no recollection of having gone to anyone's

home but his own and couldn't remember seeing Dr Dewar on April 29, let alone killing him. He denied that he had ever admitted killing the Doc.

The jury thought otherwise and found him guilty, adding a strong recommendation for mercy. Despite this recommendation, Richardson was hanged on September 7 by Thomas Pierrepoint. The famous hangman was then well over seventy and in his fortieth year as an executioner.

Following the trial, newspapers sought quotes from the numerous women who had known Dr Dewar. The most memorable came from a stripper known as Big Bertha.

"Doc," she said, "was the kindest and best man in town."

# 9

# DANGER MAN

*"I know where I'm going.*
*I'm going to Heaven."*
*Charlie Peace's final speech*

It was the end of a long day in court for secretary
Prudence Simpson. Now she was longing to get home,
make a cup of tea, put her feet up and rest her weary
head. With that thought in mind, she was hurrying
through the lobby when she bumped into a stranger. The
sheets of paper with all her trial notes skidded across the
marble floor.

With a cry of dismay, she was about to sink to her
knees and gather them up when a strong hand gripped
her shoulder. "Just leave it to me," said the stranger.

In no time at all, he had retrieved her papers. She tried
to thank him, but he would have none of that. "It was my
fault in the first place," he pointed out. "So I'm hoping
you'll allow me to make up for my clumsiness by allowing
me to walk you safely to your door. These are, after all,
dangerous times for a beautiful woman such as you to be
out there alone on the streets."

No one had ever called Prudence beautiful before; the
truth being that she was plump and rather plain. And for
that matter, it had been a long time since anyone had
offered to walk her home. So her protest was little more
than a token one and easily brushed aside.

From her position just below the bench, she had spotted the stranger seated in the front row of the public gallery for the past two days. He was quite small and not particularly handsome; but there was nevertheless a piratical look about the face, an air of derring-do, that had intrigued her. He in turn had been paying close attention to the prisoner in the dock, William Habron, who had been charged with the murder of a policeman, Constable Cock. At the conclusion of the trial, only moments earlier, Habron had been sentenced to death.

It was November, 1876, and it was snowing as they began their walk through the streets of Manchester.

"I was wondering," she said rather timidly, "why you were so interested in this trial. Is William Habron perhaps a friend or relative of yours?"

The question amused him. "I should hope not," he said, "that's a black-hearted villain if ever I saw one."

She shrugged. "I suppose you're right; but I must confess I felt a little bit sorry for him just the same."

He shook his head firmly. "Save your pity for that poor policeman he shot. These good-hearted fellows, these guardians of the law, must be protected from rogues such as that."

Somewhere along the way, he steered her into a pub and bought her a couple of brandies to keep out the cold. And when they finally reached her door, she invited him in. She was, after all, a very lonely lady.

When the morning came, she gave him breakfast. He thanked her politely and kissed her goodbye. She watched him walk away with a certain sadness, knowing that it was unlikely she'd ever see him again.

All she knew about him was that his name was Charlie, that he was a picture framer by trade and that he was an accomplished and satisfying lover.

She, of course, had no means of knowing that she had just spent the night with the man who'd shot Constable Cock. . . a man who would kill again before this day was done.

Charlie Peace was, by any standards, a remarkable criminal, quick-witted, daring and reckless; and driven on by two all-consuming passions. . . a love of danger and a love of women.

This explains why he chose to attend the murder trial of William Habron, knowing that this was the most dangerous place he could be on such a day.

This also explains why he chose Prudence Simpson for a one-night stand. Her position as court secretary gave their brief affair an added spice of danger.

It had been this way for Charlie Peace from the very beginning, possibly inherited. His father had been a one-legged liontamer and that could be a dangerous combination.

Charlie's first prison sentence, at the age of nineteen, was typical of the man. He had broken into the home of the Mayor of Sheffield. . . seemingly for Charlie, no lesser mortal would do.

He served a month's hard labour and on his release, he moved into a house with two girls, Emma James and Mary Neild. For Charlie, it was a neat arrangement. Firstly, the girls were both burglars, which meant that he became part of a ready-made team. And secondly, they were adept at three-in-a-bed sex, a pastime which appealed to Charlie.

He would boast to friends that his own sexual desires were so vast that he needed at least two women a night to satisfy them. Like many small men, he had a liking for big women; and again he'd been fortunate in his choice of partners. Emma was buxom, while Mary was tall with long legs and breasts (as Charlie put it) as firm as apples.

For a year, he lived in a burglar's paradise, waxing rich on robberies and enjoying the combined attention of his two lovers. But in 1854, his luck ran out. The three of them were arrested after they'd broken into the home of Richard Stuart, a Bradford tycoon, and stolen a large quantity of jewellery.

Charlie was sentenced to four years penal servitude.

While serving this sentence in Wakefield Prison, he escaped and climbed on to the roof of a house in the prison yard. He removed some slates and lowered himself into a bedroom. He was found later by warders, hiding on the top of a wardrobe.

This time upon his release, he searched briefly for his two previous sleeping companions, but the girls had disappeared as if off the face of the earth. But he soon found consolation in the arms of a cuddly widow named Hannah Ward.

Hannah was also a patient lady; and with Charlie Peace, she needed to be. For soon after their marriage, he was back inside again, this time serving six years.

He came out of prison as a ticket-of-leave man (a form of parole) and managed to stay out of trouble for two years. Then in 1866, he was caught red-handed 'doing a job'; and sentenced to eight years.

With each passing year, he seemed to be growing wilder; and while in Portland Prison, he headed a revolt which resulted in him being flogged with a cat o'nine tails. He was then transported to the penal fortress on Gibraltar, the home of some of Europe's most desperate criminals.

He returned to Britain in 1872 and set up a new home in Sheffield with the patient Hannah. He worked from home as a picture framer by day and as a cat burglar by night. He had become so proficient at both these crafts that it seemed just possible that he might elude the clutches of the law for the rest of his days. As a burglar, he had the ability to quieten the most ferocious dog with just a few words. He used to say that it was an art his father had handed down. . . presumably if you can control lions, dogs come easy.

This time trouble came through a different route. Charlie wasn't trying to steal jewels or money. . . just another man's wife. Initially he had become friendly with his next-door neighbours Arthur Dyson, a civil engineer, and his wife Katherine, a stunning beauty.

For a man with such a passion for women, Katherine Dyson provided a brand of temptation which Charlie Peace just couldn't resist. He courted her cleverly and, during her husband's long absences from home, they almost certainly became lovers. Charlie was now forty-three, thin and wiry, but still immensely strong. At first glance, he was far from handsome; but supposedly it was his swashbuckling ways that enabled him to make so many conquests.

Still Arthur Dyson had no wish to see Katherine added to that long list. So next time Charlie came calling, it was the husband who opened the door. "I know what you've been up to, Charlie, and I'm telling you that this ends right now. You'll never enter my house again. Is that understood?"

Charlie was reputed to have a gun with him, night and day; and without more ado he now proceeded to wave it under Mrs. Dyson's nose. "Tell your husband to go to hell," he demanded, "or else I'll blow your brains out."

The Dysons hastily slammed the door, waited until Charlie had returned to his own house and then ran to the police station. A warrant was issued for his arrest; but by the time the police arrived, Charlie and the long-suffering Hannah had fled the town.

They moved to Hull where they bought a cafe with Charlie's ill-gotten gains. He left the running of the cafe to Hannah while he continued with his life of crime, mostly by night. However he hadn't lost interest in the Dysons. He instructed his son-in-law to keep an eye on them and report any happenings.

In the meantime Charlie made the occasional trips to other towns he knew; and on the night of August 1, 1876, he went to Manchester where he selected the house of a Mr. Gratrix at Whalley Range. As he was prowling around the outside of the house, he was spotted by two policemen. The two officers split, one staying at the front of the house, the other going to the back.

Unaware of their presence, Charlie walked straight into

one of them, Constable Beanland, who made a grab for him and missed. "Stop where you are," he commanded. But Charlie did a smart about-turn and ran for it, vaulting over a low wall at the bottom of the garden.

As he landed, Charlie almost fell into the arms of the other policeman, Constable Cock. As the two men stood face to face, Charlie drew that ever-present revolver and fired two shots. The first went wide, but the second hit the officer in the chest. Cock later died from that wound. Before Beanland reached his colleague, Charlie had made good his escape.

The Manchester police, angered by the loss of one of their own, checked the movements of all major criminals in the city and soon came up with a pair of suspects, John and William Habron. Mr. Justice Lindley, as we know, eventually sentenced William Habron to death. . . a sentence fortunately commuted to life imprisonment.

In all his life, Charlie had never lived more dangerously than this. He had murdered a policeman. He had attended the trial of the man who had been mistakenly charged with that offence. And he had seduced a woman who worked alongside the dead policeman's colleagues.

One might have expected the risks he'd been taking to have sobered him for a while. In fact, they had the opposite effect. By the time he left Prudence Simpson, he was on a high, much too psyched up to return quietly to home and Hannah.

Instead he decided to visit Katherine Dyson. He arrived outside her house at about seven o'clock that evening, and waited patiently in the shadows. Eventually he saw her come out of the side of the house. He stepped in front of her and in sudden panic she dodged his outflung arm, fled and locked herself in the outside toilet. She screamed and her husband came running. He chased Charlie down the street. Then Charlie stopped running, turned and fired a shot from his revolver. That first shot missed its target; but as Dyson closed in, he fired again. The second shot hit Dyson in the temple and he died two hours later.

# A Date with the Hangman

Charlie hurried back to Hull, knowing that the police would soon be looking for him. He and his family moved overnight to London. And ten days later, a jury at Sheffield's Coroners Court brought in a verdict of wilful murder against Charles Peace.

Charlie disguised himself. He shaved off his beard, stained his face with walnut juice and started wearing spectacles. He also found himself a new mistress, Mrs. Thompson, an attractive woman known amongst her associates as 'Legs' Thompson. To complete his disguise, Charlie assumed her name. The 'Thompsons' lived in the main part of the house (a terrace in Peckham) while Hannah lived in the basement. All of which meant that Charlie was once more enjoying three-in-a-bed sex. This, remember, was an age in which any unorthodox sexual practice was considered taboo. And the fact that Charlie was able to persuade the women in his life to step across these forbidden frontiers so willingly tends to confirm the views expressed by numerous ladies after his death. He was, they said, a very accomplished lover.

For two years, he carried on his criminal activities in South London. Then on October 9, 1878, he committed his last burglary.

The target of his attention that night was a large mansion in Blackheath. He broke in easily enough and set about collecting bits of silver and placing them on a table ready for removal. But outside a policeman, PC Ted Robinson had spotted a light flickering in the drawing-room. Before investigating, he summoned the assistance of a sergeant and another officer. The sergeant ordered the two constables to go to the rear of the house; and he then walked up to the front door, knocked and rang the bell.

Charlie, a reflex man if ever there was, jumped out of the back window and ran down the garden, chased by Robinson. At the bottom of the garden, Charlie stopped, turned and aimed his revolver at the policeman.

"Keep back," he growled, "or by God, I'll shoot you."

As the policeman advanced, Charlie fired four shots at him. They all missed and before he could fire again, Robinson punched him in the face. Charlie staggered backwards, saying, "You bugger, I'll settle you this time."

He fired a fifth shot which hit the constable in the right arm. But the plucky Robinson tackled him with one arm and, after a terrific struggle, Charlie was arrested and charged with attempted murder.

He gave his name as John Ward and he was tried under that name at the Old Bailey in November, 1878 before Mr. Justice Hawkins. The trial was brief and the jury didn't even bother to leave the court. 'John Ward' was found guilty and sentenced to life imprisonment.

Now that Charlie was inside, Legs Thompson was beginning to feel the pinch. There were no more presents (Charlie had always been generous to the women in his life). . . no more nights of passion. . . and even worse, no money. So she decided to cash in on the £100 reward that was on offer for the capture of Charles Frederick Peace. She informed the police that the John Ward serving life in Pentonville was in fact the Charles Frederick Peace wanted for murder in Sheffield.

On January 22, 1879, Charlie was taken by train from King's Cross to Sheffield. Then as the train approached the outskirts of Sheffield, the prisoner made a last desperate bid for freedom by diving head first through the carriage window. Charlie landed on the tracks and suffered only minor injuries but he was soon overpowered and recaptured. Eventually he reached Sheffield where his police escort had to run the gauntlet of a large and angry crowd, all baying for Charlie's blood.

He was tried for the murder of Arthur Dyson at the Leeds Assizes on February 4, 1879. The judge was the Honourable Mr. Justice Lopes. Mr. Campbell Foster led for the Crown and Charlie was defended by Mr. Frank Lockwood.

Mr. Lockwood felt that Charlie had just one slim chance; and that this would be to discredit Katherine

Dyson. He set out to prove that she had been having an affair with Charlie. In all probability this was true, but it failed to sway the jury one iota. They found Charlie guilty of wilful murder after a ten-minute deliberation. The judge donned the black cap and sentenced him to death.

Charlie accepted the sentence with a smile that looked genuine enough; but at this point, the court secretary fainted and had to be revived with smelling salts. Her name: Prudence Simpson!

In the death cell, Charlie asked to see the Rev J. Littlewood, Vicar of Darnall. "I just wanted to do the decent thing," he told the vicar, "and make a confession. I'm the man who shot PC Cock to death and poor Bill Habron is now in prison serving a sentence for something he didn't do."

As a result of that confession, Habron was given a free pardon and awarded £1,000 as compensation, a considerable sum in those days.

At eight o'clock on February 25, 1879, Charlie was led to the gallows erected in a yard behind Leeds Prison. It was a bitterly cold morning and the ground was covered with a layer of snow. There were four reporters present, which had become the custom after the abolition of public executions in 1868.

Charlie seemed remarkably cheerful, almost as though he was relishing this his final starring role. He made a short speech, saying, "My last thoughts are for my children and their mother, a wonderful woman. They musn't worry about me I know where I'm going. I'm going to Heaven."

The executioner was William Marwood, a shoemaker from Lincolnshire. As he drew the hood over Charlie's head, the murderer asked for a drink of water. And then just as Marwood sprang the trap, Charlie was heard to say, "Amen, God bless you all."

Marwood was over fifty years old before he became a hangman, and he soon became well known all over Britain. He was called 'The Gentleman Hangman,' and

the children had a riddle about him;
"If Pa killed Ma, who'd kill Pa?"
"Mawood."

Following the death of Charlie, Katherine Dyson became something of a celebrity. She received several proposals of marriage, was offered a number of engagements at music halls and invited to write her life story. She refused all these offers and sailed off to America to begin a new life.

# 10

# A HANGMAN'S TALE

*"Harry, I wish I had never come."*
*James Billington's last words to*
*fellow executioner Henry Pierrepoint.*

There was pandemonium in the room as neighbours milled around the severely wounded Anna McKenna. And only one man seemingly had remained calm in the crisis. William Billington had placed his strong right arm around Mrs. McKenna's shoulders and was holding a cloth against her throat with his left hand in a bid to staunch the flow.

"Just relax, Anna," he was saying. "The doctor will be here soon. You're going to be all right." But he knew this wasn't really true. She had already lost too much blood and was fading fast.

She spoke and he had to bend his head to hear the words. "Please, Bill, don't let me die," she whispered.

"I won't luv," he said gently. And in that very moment, her body gave one final shudder and she died in his arms.

He kissed her brow gently. "What kind of man," he asked, "could do such a thing to such a woman?"

There were tears in his eyes and that fact would have come as a surprise to many; for Bill Billington was no stranger to death. With his father James and brothers John and Tommy, he was part of a famous family of executioners.

74

It was said by their detractors that if they'd wept every time they'd seen someone die, they would have been forever weeping.

James had answered that charge by stating, "We reserve our tears for the victims."

Still it was rare for murder to become quite so personal as this. The Billingtons were neighbours of the McKennas and knew them well. And this time, there was no mystery to solve. Pat McKenna had been searching for his wife in a drunken rage. She had taken refuge in her daughter-in-law's house, but he had found her and then stabbed her to death.

The local bobby, PC Spencer, arrived to find Anna already dead; but neighbours told him that Pat McKenna had been seen entering his own house just a few doors away. Spencer went to the house and found him hiding in the coalhole under the stairs. He had a knife and a clay pipe in his hand and appeared to be very drunk. He was arrested without a struggle and taken to the Town Hall.

During the journey, he said, "I'm sorry it happened. I went to the house without premeditation or malice. She dared me twice before I did it. She put the knife on the table and said, 'If you want to do it, do it.' It was done in a minute."

On Wednesday, November 13, 1901, 53-year-old Pat McKenna stepped into the dock at the Manchester Assizes. His face gave the impression that his few weeks in prison had been a trying experience. He was haggard and anxious.

The Clerk of the Assize, Sir Hubert Stephen, read out the indictment to McKenna, who cupped his hand to his ear and strained to hear the words. At this, defence counsel Mr. T.C. Gibbons informed Mr. Justice Bucknill that his client was very deaf. McKenna eventually pleaded not guilty and Mr. Sutton rose to open the case for the prosecution.

However before he could speak, the judge said to the crowded court, "I am sorry to see that there are children here today. There is a boy over there who is not a witness. Take him out. There is a girl of about five in the gallery – let her go out too. I hope those looking after the doors will not admit children of such ages. I will not have them here listening to murder cases. It is bad enough to see women in court, but children. . ."

It was the daughter-in-law, Emma McKenna, who outlined the background to the case for the benefit of the court. She explained that at the turn of the century, master joiner Pat McKenna had lost his job and been unable to find another. So with money running short, his wife took in lodgers, a Mr. and Mrs. Palmer, to supplement their income. At first the arrangement worked well, then Pat McKenna became obsessed with the idea that Mr. Palmer was having an affair with his wife. From then on the domestic happiness of the McKennas was shattered, and their home became a place of constant friction.

McKenna sought solace in the many public houses in the area, spending money that should have gone towards the housekeeping. The Derby Hotel, run by James Billington, was one of his favourite watering holes.

In her struggle to make ends meet, Anna was forced to visit the pawnbrokers; and on that fateful day, her husband demanded some of the money. When she refused, he threatened her so violently that she decided to hide in her daughter-in-law's house for the rest of the day. Several times during the next few hours, he knocked on the door seeking his wife; and each time he was told that she wasn't there.

But he returned yet again at five o'clock and on this occasion he looked through the window and spotted Anna in the front room. She ran into the back room, but was dragged into the kitchen by her husband.

Emma McKenna continued, "I had just used a knife to cut some meat and placed it on the table. He picked it up and said to my mother-in-law that he would cut her throat. I took the knife away from him, but he picked it up again and stabbed her in the neck. I ran out to get help, but on returning I found that he had gone. Poor Anna was slouched in the chair with blood pouring from her mouth."

Mr. Gibbons asked her to describe the prisoner's character prior to the moment when he lost his job.

She replied, "He was normally a good and sober man. But after losing his job, he took to drink; and when drunk, it was as though he was mad."

Did she think it possible that her mother-in-law had been having an affair with Mr. Palmer?

She shook her head firmly. "The very thought of such a thing is ridiculous," she said. "Only Pat KcKenna when drunk could have dreamed of such a thing."

There were no witnesses for the defence. Mr. Gibbons told the jury that they had now heard the full story; and so the fate of the accused rested in their hands. It was their decision as to whether he should live or die. It was either murder and death by hanging; or manslaughter and life, although this might mean a long existence in prison.

It would be futile, he said, for the defence to suggest that the prisoner should have his liberty; because the dead woman clearly met her death at his hands. However he did ask the jury to say that the case was one of manslaughter. . . which was killing in law, but not under circumstances similar to those found in the capital offence. This would permit the accused to live out the allotted span of his life given to him by God.

Mr. Justice Bucknill asked the jury to dismiss from their minds the question of insanity. The only question before them was: did the accused commit the murder with malice aforethought?

He had the reputation of being a humane judge and this showed as he said, "If you can find anything in the evidence which will induce you to arrive at a verdict of manslaughter, no one will be more delighted than me. But this is such a serious charge that you must be quite satisfied in your hearts that there is very genuine evidence in favour of such a view."

After half an hour's deliberation, the jury returned a verdict of wilful murder. McKenna was asked whether he had anything to say and, looking straight at the judge, he said, "My Lord, there has been talk about my wife, and talk about me being jealous of her. That had never entered my mind at all. I now want to clear her name. She was as good a woman as was ever married and tied to a man."

Wearing the black cap, the judge told McKenna, "You have been found guilty on the clearest of evidence. However I was glad to hear the remarks you've just made in the dock. It has probably given relief to your mind, and by so doing you have cleared your dead wife of that which might otherwise have stained her character. Sadly, I can't give you any hope in this world. You must forfeit your life and I beg you to prepare yourself for that terrible moment."

McKenna never expected a reprieve, but his friends worked hard on his behalf. A petition was signed by over thirty thousand people, including the Mayor of Bolton, local MP's and the magistrates who had committed him for trial; but the Home Office could find no grounds for granting a reprieve.

James Billington and Henry Pierrepoint were chosen to carry out the execution, and arrived at Strangeways on the afternoon of Monday, December 2, 1901. For James Billington, who knew McKenna so well, this promised to be a considerable ordeal. That night in the prison, James was taken ill; but he insisted upon carrying out his task. He was no better the following morning, and Pierrepoint had to help him dress.

Hangmen such as Billington and Pierrepoint took considerable pride in their expertise. Although they had a poor opinion of murderers en masse, they nevertheless took great pains to dispatch them into the next world as swiftly and as painlessly as possible. This was why James

Billington was so insistent upon playing his part in the execution. As Pat McKenna had been both a neighbour and a customer in his bar, he felt that it was his duty to help him through what the judge had described as "that terrible moment."

McKenna was crying bitterly as Billington entered the condemned cell. He must have recognised the hangman, but he was so upset that he made no sign. The scaffold was only a few feet away from the cell and the distance was soon covered. Quicker than it takes to tell, his head was placed in the noose, his feet strapped, and the lever pulled to plunge McKenna six feet seven inches to his death.

Billington managed to control himself throughout the execution, but he was ill again soon afterwards. Pierrepoint had to help him to the station and on to the train.

As Pierrepoint made his friend comfortable in the carriage, the older man turned and said, "Harry, I wish I had never come."

Those were the last words he ever spoke to Pierrepoint, for ten days later, Billington died in his Bolton home. Thus his sons, William, John and Tommy, took over much of his work load, as they carried on this family tradition of hangmen.

But the McKenna case was unique in its way. . . being the only occasion upon which the Billingtons shed tears for victim and killer alike.

# 11

# THE SIXTH SENSE

*"Never trust a smiler."*
*Superintendent Ball's advice*
*to his sergeant.*

The church caretaker was a very equable man, which was perhaps just as well. His father, you see, had been something of a homegrown comedian. He had thought it would be highly amusing to give his son a name that would match his surname . . . a joke to carry through life and to remind him of his good old laugh-a-minute dad. So he christened him Albert Hall.

Certainly his schoolmates had considered this incredibly funny, a continual source of wisecracks. Albert too had been mildly amused at first; but after the hundredth joke, the humour had begun to pall a little . . . and very soon the whole affair had become a pain in the neck. But he never said so. Very early in life, he had learnt that a smile is the perfect shield to be used against the vagaries of the world. This philosophy had carried him smoothly through his school days, through his days in the air force and as a butler too. Now, only two days into his new job as caretaker at the Park Lane Congregational Church in Halifax, he was once again needing to be an equable man.

A six-year-old girl called Mary Hackett, whose home

faced the church, had disappeared; and the police were mounting one of the most thorough searches ever known in the north. Post Office workers, a mountain rescue team, even Scouts and Girl Guides searched moorlands and woods around the perimeter of Halifax. Special constables had been drafted in to assist the regular police search the town itself. And now even the crypt of the church was being searched by officers in muddy hobnailed boots who had just come off the moors.

They were moving pews and chairs willy-nilly. And as Albert Hall watched, he wondered ruefully just how long it would take him to restore the crypt to its previous pristine condition. But he didn't utter a word of complaint. That wasn't in his nature. Instead he made them a pot of tea; and when they apologised for the mess they'd made, he gave them his smile.

"Don't you worry about that," he said. "You just concentrate upon finding that poor girl, and pray God you find her alive."

As the days and the weeks rolled by, the chances of such a happy ending diminished steadily. The Chief Constable, Mr. G. Goodman, realising that every line of inquiry had been exhausted, called in Scotland Yard; and help arrived in the burly form of Detective Superintendent John Ball and Detective Sergeant Dennis Hawkins.

The superintendent, a painstaking man, decided to retrace the steps already taken in the hope that some new clue would emerge. So he had the crypt searched again.

Albert Hall, although he may have sighed inwardly, was outwardly his normal equable self. He made another pot of tea, produced a tin of biscuits and said to John Ball, "I only wish I could help you more. But as you doubtless know, I only arrived here two days before this unfortunate girl disappeared and so I never even had the chance to talk to her."

He spoke freely to the two detectives and couldn't have been more cooperative. However Ball wasn't impressed.

As they left the church, he turned to Sergeant Hawkins and said, "I think we shall keep an eye on Mr. Hall."

Hawkins was intrigued. "For any particular reason?" he asked.

The superintendent shrugged. "He smiles too much," he said. "Never trust a smiler."

That hunch, that sixth sense, call it what you will, stayed with John Ball. He had the former butler placed under surveillance, followed wherever he went. The police kept a day and night record of his movements for a month; but in that time he did nothing at all to justify Ball's suspicions.

Even so, the superintendent decided to search the crypt yet again. The search proved to be every bit as fruitless as the ones that had gone before. The caretaker was as friendly as ever, chatting non-stop and eager to please.

Ball pointed out to him that two pots of paint standing on a pile of chairs in one corner of the crypt hadn't been sealed. "I should pop the lids on, if I was you," he said to Albert Hall, "otherwise they'll dry up."

The caretaker laughed. "My guess is that they've already been thrown away. I fear, my friend, that I'm not a very practical man."

He frequently referred to the Scotland Yard men as "my friends" and it was almost as though he welcomed their visits. And this time as they left, the superintendent thought for a moment that he had seen a look of fleeting triumph in the caretaker's eyes. Or was he perhaps becoming paranoiac about this seemingly harmless man . . . allowing that sixth sense to colour his judgment?

Almost six weeks had gone by since the disappearance of Mary Hackett and his own frustration was growing all the while. He began to review the case slowly and then he remembered the two pots of paint. He asked himself whether any man, however careless, could actually lose two lids. And if they hadn't been lost, what purpose would it serve to leave the pots open? Could it be that the paint fumes were intended to cover up some other smell?

He decided to make a fourth and final search of the crypt. He immediately ordered up arc-lights, a posse of policemen, firemen and labourers armed with picks and shovels.

At the head of this army, he arrived at the church; and this time, Albert Hall was no longer an equable man. His usual friendly greeting gave way to anger as he saw the size of the party.

He shouted, "You have no right to come digging and I am not going to let you in."

The two Scotland Yard men brushed him aside. The chairs were moved away from the corner where the paint pots stood and the digging began, slowly and carefully. After half an hour, part of a human leg had been uncovered. The digging was stopped and Home Office pathologist Dr Price was sent for. Then the work of brushing away the soil continued; and in just over an hour, the body of the missing Mary Hackett was exposed and taken away to the mortuary. The child's parents identified the body from the clothes, as the face was unrecognisable. It was revealed at the post-mortem that she had seven small wounds on her scalp and a big hole in the back of her skull. There had been no sexual interference.

All this posed something of a dilemma for the superintendent. He was by now quite sure in his own mind that Albert Hall had murdered the small girl, but he still lacked any positive proof. So he made no move to arrest the caretaker and simply increased the surveillance in the belief that, if guilty, Hall would eventually betray himself.

The very next day, Hall left the church and set off through the streets of the town, shadowed all the way. After leaving the outskirts of Halifax, he went into the grounds of a large building. The sign over the gate read: Scalebor Park Hospital. The local detectives explained to John Ball that this was an asylum, a home for the mentally disturbed.

The superintendent waited until the caretaker had left and then paid his own visit to the asylum. He was told that Hall had spoken to a Dr Valentine.

At first, the doctor was reluctant to disclose any details of the conversation But once he realised that this was a murder investigation, he told the superintendent that this had indeed been the reason why the caretaker had come to see him. He wanted to convince the doctor that he'd had nothing to do with the death of the little girl.

He had then made what was to prove a fatal mistake. He had given the doctor details about the injuries that only the killer could have known, as the police hadn't as yet released any information.

Ball asked Dr Valentine why the caretaker had chosen to make this visit to him rather than anybody else. The doctor looked surprised. "Didn't you know?" he said. "He used to be a patient here."

Albert Hall continued to treat the superintendent as his friend and made over thirty voluntary statements. On September 24, Ball decided he had enough evidence and so he charged him with murder.

The caretaker shrugged almost casually. "Very well," he said. "I have been expecting this."

The trial was held in March, 1954, before Mr. Justice Pearson. The Crown was led by Mr. H.B.H. Hylton-Foster and Albert Hall was represented by Mr. Rudolph Lyons. From a legal point of view, the case was interesting because there was no direct evidence against Hall, forensic or otherwise. The jury were being asked to convict him solely on the strength of his own statements.

He spent three and a half hours in the witness box. He was pale, but gave his evidence in a composed way. He was asked how he was able to describe the girl's injuries to Dr Valentine during that visit to the asylum.

He replied, "Sergeant Hawkins gave me the details when we spoke at the police station on the day the body had been discovered."

He was asked what time of day this conversation had

taken place and he replied, "Somewhere around one o'clock."

Mr. Hylton-Foster then pointed out to him that the sergeant hadn't been anywhere near the station at that time. After the body had been found, he had been sent away from the church to make inquiries elsewhere. Furthermore no one knew the precise injuries until Dr Price had concluded his examination at 3.15 p.m. that day. This was the key feature of the prosecution's case.

On the fourth day, the jury retired at 4.17 p.m. into a dressing room under the stage of the Town Hall. Four hours later, they still hadn't reached a verdict; so they were moved to another room, because a band was due to play on the stage right above them.

Another two and a half hours went by and then finally the jury returned with a verdict of guilty.

When asked whether he had anything to say, Hall said, "My Lord, I am not guilty of this crime. It is a terrible crime, I admit, but I am not guilty of it. I must thank you, my Lord, for conducting this trial in the best of . . . ."

His voice became so quiet that no one was able to pick up the end of that speech.

He listened to the death sentence impassively and that habitual smile returned fleetingly as he nodded and turned to leave the dock. He was hanged on April 22 by Steve Wade.

Two factors were responsible for his downfall:

1. His own willingness to talk. He was eventually condemned by his own words.

2. The sixth sense of a policeman who distrusted smilers.

Several years later, the file on the Mary Hackett murder was reopened after a man had confessed to being the real killer. But after an investigation, the file was closed again . . . with the police seemingly quite confident that the confession was bogus.

# 12

# THE GANGBUSTER

*"You've done our kind and now we'll do you."*
*Lawrence Fowler's threat to William Plommer.*

Trimmer Welsh, the strongarm man for the Fowler gang, walked into the Black Swan and an uneasy silence settled over the tap-room. A space along the bar opened up as if by magic; for the Trimmer, a sixteen-stone powerhouse, had a fearsome reputation. He enjoyed violence for violence's sake and on Saturday nights such as this, he would cruise through the Sheffield pubs, the eternal hunter seeking victims to hammer with his rocklike fists. And at such times, just about any man would do. But tonight it seemed as though the men in the Black Swan could relax a little. The Trimmer had sighted a different sort of quarry, the pub's new barmaid.

Carmen Esteban was Spanish and in the mid-twenties Europeans were seldom seen in Sheffield. There was beauty in her face and boldness too. But it was really her figure which caught the eye. For at nineteen, her body was already ripe to overflowing, which was of course one of the reasons she had found employment as a barmaid so easy to find.

She was talking to Bill Plommer, an ex-fighter who'd once had a big following in the city. He was a quietly-spoken Scot, well liked by his neighbours, and probably the only man in the pub that night who wasn't remotely scared of the Trimmer. To the Trimmer, this lack of fear came as a personal affront. And as he watched Plommer and Carmen, heads close together, he was touched by anger.

The pub's regular barman Charlie was waiting to serve him; but the Trimmer turned instead to Carmen. "Get me a pint, girl," he said loudly, "that is if you can spare the time from talking to your fancy man."

The bar was suddenly silent, all eyes on Plommer. There was just a hint of a smile on the ex-fighter's face, but he said nothing. He had seen this game played out too many times before. Carmen, startled, was about to respond, but Plommer's calm assurance stopped her. So with a touch of style beyond her years, she poured two leisurely pints, handing the first to Plommer and the second to the Trimmer, but only after a considerable delay.

The Trimmer surveyed her slowly, allowing his gaze to linger lewdly over hip and breast. Then he turned to Plommer. "Are you the fancy man or just the ponce?" he asked, well aware that in the twenties these were the most insulting terms of all.

He looked closely at Plommer and everyone else looked too; but again the ex-fighter just shrugged and said nothing. You could sense the disappointment in the pub, but there was understanding too. Ten years had gone by since he quit the ring and the Trimmer outweighed him by the best part of three stone.

"You see," said the Trimmer turning back to Carmen, "you're surrounded by cowards," and raising his glass, he added, "and I'm not paying for froth. Tip it out and pour me another."

Carmen, too young and too innocent to have experienced fear, shook her head firmly. "It's the same as everyone else's. So drink it up and enough of this nonsense."

The Trimmer's game had almost run its course. "Change it," he growled, "or I'm coming over the bar to learn you a few manners."

At this, Plommer spoke for the first time. "Be careful," was all he said. And the Trimmer, who lived in a world where the loudest is king, was the only one to miss the menace in that quiet voice. Maybe he was concentrating too hard on Carmen who had totally ignored him. She was just about to serve another customer when he threw his drink in her face ... It was the beer dripping down and staining her favourite dress that seemed to anger her the most.

"You bastard," she cried.

The Trimmer was starting to climb the bar when Plommer put a restraining hand upon his chest, pushing him back a pace. The Trimmer looked at that hand on his chest, clearly astonished that anyone should dare to place it there. He knocked it aside and in the same movement threw his big right hand.

Although ten years had gone by since the days of Plommer's glory, some things never go away. He swayed aside from the punch almost lazily; and then as the Trimmer's weight carried him forward; the ex-fighter caught him with two ferocious punches to the head, a left hook followed by a right cross. The big man was out long before he hit the floor; but just to make sure Plommer brought up his knee, pulping the Trimmer's nose for good measure.

The other drinkers, no longer afraid, came to stare down at the ruins of a face. They carried the Trimmer out of the Black Swan on a door; and it took eight strong men to bear the burden.

At police headquarters, Inspector Percy Sillitoe heard the news of the fight within the hour and he was delighted. He was a big, burly man who was reputed to be totally fearless. So it came as no surprise when he was placed in charge of a special gangbusting squad. Organised crime in the city had been running riot, threatening to turn this Yorkshire town into a mini-version of Chicago. He had hand-picked an elite squad, all of them as fearless as himself. They had infiltrated the gangs, discovered their secrets and yet remained frustrated. As in their Chicago counterpart, the citizens were running scared, refusing to take a stand. And until there were men brave enough to come into court and testify, the gangs would continue to run free.

This was why the news of the Trimmer's downfall came as such welcome news. Sillitoe summoned his squad and told them, "This is what we've been waiting for. Now that one man had been game enough to stand up to the Fowlers, the tide will start to turn. The honest citizens will realise that there is nothing very special about these thugs. If the Trimmer can be taken, they can all be taken. Most of them are cowards at heart and you can be sure none of them will be game enough to take on Plommer single-handed."

He chuckled. "Mind you, I don't blame them. I've seen Bill Plommer in the ring and I've never known a harder or a gamer man. He just wouldn't know how to run. Once this news gets around, he'll have half the city behind him. We'll get our witnesses and then we'll finally break these gangs who stain the good name of the city."

One of the squad asked Sillitoe, "Sir, what do you expect the Fowlers to do now?"

"Oh, they'll go after Plommer mob-handed," he replied matter-of-factly. "They've no choice. They've got to, otherwise they're finished. And as soon as they do, we've got to be ready to make our own move."

Trouble came two nights later. Plommer and another boxer named Jack Clay were approached by Wilfred Fowler – at twenty-three, the younger of the Fowler brothers – and two members of his gang.

Wilfred had been drinking, but he was still sober enough to pick on Clay, whom he considered to be the softer option. He warned, "Stay away from Jock (Plommer was Scottish). Otherwise we'll do you too. No one messes with the Fowlers." And so saying, he threw a punch which Clay blocked easily enough.

Plommer was amused. "Give the boy a tanning, Jack," he said, "and I'll keep these other two monkeys off your back."

Clay proceeded to give Wilfred a methodical beating, while his two henchmen watched helplessly . . . too scared of Plommer to intervene.

The fight stopped when Wilfred could no longer stand on his feet. His men picked him up and he stood there for a moment with his arms draped around their shoulders. He turned to Plommer and said, "Jock, you've got a tanning coming for this."

Plommer shrugged. "Go home, Wilfred," he said. "You don't look much like a winner to me."

It was April 26, 1925, and Bill Plommer had less than twenty-four hours left to live.

The following evening he was sitting in his house in Princess Street when his ten-year-old son Tommy returned home with some cigarettes for him.

"Dad," he said breathlessly, "there's a gang of men out there in the street looking for you."

Plommer calmly picked up his cap and went outside. As soon as he stepped on to the street, he was surrounded by nine members of the Fowler gang. A neighbour, Mrs. Hannah Beever, called out, "Jock, if I were you, I'd run."

Plommer remained as calm as ever. "I'll not run," he said. "I'll fight them singly and I'll beat the lot of them."

But he wasn't to be given that chance. The gang attacked him instantly. He was stabbed, kicked, thumped and hit with chains and truncheons. The Fowlers then scattered and Plommer staggered home with blood gushing from wounds in his chest, stomach and head.

The police arrived and found him slumped in a chair, but still conscious. He was taken to hospital, where he died an hour later from his wounds.

His death had a remarkable effect on the city. He became an overnight hero. Men who had been prepared to stand on the sidelines were suddenly ashamed that they had allowed this one man to stand alone against the mobs. On the day of his funeral, crowds standing twelve-deep lined the two-mile route from Princess Street to the Burngreave Cemetery, where an estimated eight thousand mourners waited. The coffin was draped with the Union Jack.

Meanwhile Percy Sillitoe and his squad had gone into

action, hunting down the Fowlers. They were as rough and ruthless in their own way as the men they pursued; and several of the eleven men arrested had been severely battered. This time Sillitoe the Gangbuster had his witnesses, men only too willing to make a stand against the mob.

The trial took place before Mr. Justice Finlay and lasted four days. The prosecution was led by Mr. G.F.L. Mortimer.

Police Constable Daniel Hagen, one of Sillitoe's men, told the court that he had arrived in Princess Street soon after the fight, and seen some men sitting on the doorstep of a fish and chip shop. Among them were the two brothers, Lawrence and Wilfred Fowler. Lawrence had a poker in his left hand and a razor in his right, both covered in blood.

Wilfred's thumb had been cut and his brother said to Hagen, "Look what they've done to him. They've nearly cut his thumb off."

Hagen asked who "they" were and Lawrence replied, "Jock, the steward at the club."

Witnesses who had been in Princess Street that night told a very different story. Lawrence had been heard to say, "You've done our kid and now we'll do you." He had then been seen to jab something at Plommer's stomach. Witness after witness identified some or all of the defendants as the men who attacked Plommer.

On the third day of the trial, four of the accused were discharged on the direction of the judge. The case continued against the remaining seven.

Both the Fowlers gave evidence and claimed that Plommer had started the fight. Lawrence said that on that fateful day he'd gone to the races at Uttoxeter. He had returned to Sheffield in the evening and learnt that a challenge had been thrown out for a fight between Wilfred and Plommer. He went with his brother to see Plommer and arrange the fight. When they arrived in Princess Street, they'd been met by Plommer who had a poker in one hand and a razor in the other. Before a word passed between the three men, Plommer hit both the brothers with the poker. Lawrence admitted that he and his brother hit Palmer, but only in self-defence. They didn't use any weapons. Neither of the brothers could remember any more details, because they were stunned and dazed after being hit with the poker.

The story made no attempt to explain the stab wounds suffered by the deceased; and to some extent it showed just how arrogant the gangsters had become. Without men brave enough to stand up and witness against them, they had been able to concoct the flimsiest tales. . . confident that the police couldn't prove a case against them. Now, thanks to Bill Plommer, everything had changed.

Juries had also been known to buckle under the threats posed by the gangs. . . but not this one. They returned verdicts of guilty of murder against the Fowlers (Lawrence and Wilfred), guilty of manslaughter against George Willis, Amos Stewart and Stanley Harker; and not guilty against Fred Goddard and Sam Garvin, who were released. Willis and Stewart were sentenced to ten years penal servitude, Harker to seven years.

The Fowlers were asked by the clerk of the court whether they had anything to say before sentence of death was passed. Wilfred said nothing, but his brother turned towards the public gallery and shouted, "If Jock Plommer's wife had told the truth, this court would know I was innocent."

The judge then told the jury, "I rejoice that you have found it possible to return these verdicts." This was a further reminder of the power the gangs had hitherto exerted over the citizens of Sheffield. As a reward, he granted them exemption from further jury service for seven years.

Wilfred Fowler was hanged in Leeds Prison on September 3, 1925, alongside Alfred Bostock, the Rotherham murderer. Lawrence Fowler was hanged the following day. Thomas Pierrepoint was the executioner on both occasions.

It would appear that the toughs of Sheffield were scared off by the prospect of ending up on the Armley scaffold, and the gangs of the city broke up. Inspector Sillitoe's band of no-nonsense bobbies returned to their normal duties and peace returned to this South Yorkshire town.

Percy Sillitoe's work however wasn't over. He was eventually promoted to Chief Constable and sent to Glasgow, where he adopted the same tactics to tame the Scottish gangs.

He was much admired by fellow officers and citizens alike. And he in turn continued to admire the man who had been brave enough to stand alone, a dead hero named Bill Plommer.

He once said, "In Sheffield, Bill Plommer deserves to be remembered as 'The Gangbuster', not me."

# 13

# THE HALF-PINT

*"Yes, sir, I'm pregnant." Louie Calvert's
reply when asked by the clerk of the court whether
she had anything to say before
the sentence was announced.*

As a lady of the streets, she had just committed a cardinal
error. She had provided a service without first collecting
what the Church were wont to call the ill-gotten gains.
Now the client and the whore, both stark naked, were
standing on opposite sides of the bed, debating the
matter.

The client, a pompous salesman, was smug with the
satisfaction of the conman who has just seen another mug
bite the dust. "I forgot to bring my wallet today," he was
saying. "So I'm afraid you'll have to wait until next time."
And both of them, of course, knew that there would never
be a next time.

He was wise enough in the ways of the world to know
that this could be a dangerous game to play with the
wrong woman. But Louie Gomersall was so diminutive,
less than five feet tall and with the face and figure of a
schoolgirl, that he had no worries. It was, he told himself,
like taking candy from a baby.

However this baby was quick on her feet. Without so
much as a word, she seized his trousers from the chair at

the foot of the bed and threw them out of the window.

He arrived in time to see them floating away on the wind to be greeted by cheers and shrieks of laughter from the girls who lined the street below, fellow members of the fraternity.

"You stupid bitch," he yelled, "why did you do that? I told you I'd pay next time."

She didn't bother to tell him that she'd heard that line somewhere before. She simply opened the top drawer of her bedside cabinet and took out a cut-throat razor.

"Now, you bugger," she said, "you've got a choice. You either pay me or I'll take my pound of flesh." She was looking at his loins in a very meaningful manner indeed.

He had always prided himself upon being streetwise and so he looked into her eyes, hoping to see the tell-tale signs of bluff. Instead he saw a desire for violence that unnerved him. Her hand, he noticed, was as steady as the proverbial rock. He wondered how he could ever have looked upon her as a schoolgirl.

"All right," he said hastily, "I'll give you your money. But first you'll have to fetch my trousers. The wallet's in the back pocket."

She smiled and yet there was no humour in that smile. "Oh no," she said, "you're going to do the fetching and then you're going to bring the money back to me."

He shrugged, as though accepting the inevitable. "Give me my shirt then," he said, "and I'll fetch you your pound."

The smile went away. "What kind of fool do you take me for?" she asked. "You walk out there in your shirt and you'd slip your breeches on and be away. No, you're going out the way you are, buck naked." She paused, "Unless, of course, you want to try and get your shirt!" The hand holding the razor rose. The eyes were eager.

So without too much choice in the matter, he fetched his trousers. . . being forced to run the gauntlet of the other girls who had played this game before.

With his pride affronted, he went to complain at the local police station in Leeds, much to the amusement of the grizzled desk sergeant. Having listened to the story, the sergeant asked him whether he knew her name.

"No, I don't," replied the salesman, "but she's easy to spot. She's tiny and could be mistaken for a schoolkid, until you take a good look at her eyes. There can't be too many girls like that in Bond Street."

The sergeant was laughing. "There aren't," he said. "That's Louie Gomersall. We call her 'Half-Pint' and maybe you're lucky, maybe you got away more lightly than you deserve. That one's a wild one, I can tell you. Once her dander's up, she'll stop at nothing."

The salesman was growing angry. "Well, what are you going to do about it?" he asked.

"Nothing," replied the sergeant matter-of-factly. "The only offence committed was your refusal to pay your dues. And believe me, with that one, you were very, very lucky. Take my advice and stay well away from her in the future. She's dangerous."

That was the reputation Louie Gomersall had in Leeds during the Twenties; and despite her size, she was truly feared by those who knew her. As a prostitute, she was reasonably successful. . . largely because of that diminutive build. Even at thirty, she still had the look of a teenager and so fitted neatly into the dreams of the kind of men who were forever seeking the young ones.

But early in 1925, she went as housekeeper to a night-watchman called Arthur Calvert, a pleasant kindly man who wasn't overwise in the ways of women. She had decided that, at thirty-two, she needed a more stable line of work. She had also decided that it would be a smart idea to marry Arthur Calvert. So after she had been with him for six months, she told him (falsely) that she was pregnant; and on August 5, they were married.

As the months rolled by without any signs of the coming baby, Arthur naturally became suspicious. Instead of telling her husband she'd been mistaken, Louie hatched a plot to obtain a new-born baby and pass it off as her own.

She showed him a letter supposedly written by her sister in Dewsbury who was inviting Louie to stay with her during the confinement. Needless to say, she had written the letter herself.

Next day, she set off for Dewsbury where she stayed just long enough to send Arthur a telegram, informing him of her safe arrival. She then doubled back to her old happy hunting ground, Bond Street in Leeds.

In Bond Street just about anything could be obtained for a price, including lodgings; and Louie soon found these with an old friend named Lily Waterhouse. As soon as she moved in, she placed an advertisement in the *Yorkshire Evening News* which read: 'Wanted: to adopt baby girl from birth. Good home offered.' A mother whose young teenage daughter had just given birth to a little girl answered the advert and Louie agreed to adopt the baby.

But meanwhile life in the Waterhouse domain hadn't been running smoothly. Several items had disappeared and Mrs. Waterhouse had no doubts about the culprit. She knew Louie of old. She also knew of that fiery temper and that willingness to resort to violence. Too scared to accuse Louie face to face, she went instead to the police who arranged for her to take out a summons the following day, Thursday, April 1, 1926.

She went home, convinced that her worries would soon be over. The police had assured her that once the summons had been served, her now unwelcome guest would be forced to leave.

Lily Waterhouse was seen going into her house at five-thirty that evening, and that was the last time she was seen alive. Soon after seven, a neighbour heard strange sounds coming from Lily's back bedroom. The neighbour continued to watch the house and soon afterwards the door opened and out stepped Louie carrying a baby wrapped in a shawl, a bag and a handbag.

The neighbour asked whether Lily was still in the house and Louie replied casually enough, "Oh, yes, I have just left her in bed. She's crying because I'm leaving her."

Later that evening, she returned to her own home. Arthur Calvert was delighted to see his wife and new baby daughter. They had a small party to celebrate the event and decided to name the little girl Dorothy.

When Arthur came downstairs the following morning, he spotted a strange suitcase in the living-room. "Whose portmanteau is this?" he asked.

Louie shrugged. "My sister in Dewsbury gave it to me," she said. "It's full of baby clothes."

It was April Fool's day and, as far as Louie was concerned, the day had been aptly named; for she had committed a series of incredible blunders.

When Lily Waterhouse failed to appear in court to take out her summons, the police went to her house to discover the reason why. The door was locked and the curtains were still drawn even though this was the middle of the afternoon. So considering this suspicious, they obtained a key and let themselves in. They found Lily lying dead on the floor of the small back bedroom. She was as stiff as the proverbial board. Her head had been battered almost beyond recognition, and the wall close to the bed was splattered with blood. The police surgeon fixed the time of death as about seven o'clock the previous evening . . . just around the time when Louie had been seen leaving the house.

The police also found a letter addressed to Louie Calvert, written in pencil. It was the letter she had written to herself. . . the letter she claimed had come from her sister in Dewsbury. This was the first of the blunders which came to roost that day. Due to her record of violence and the pending summons, Louie was already a prime suspect. But that letter left so carelessly in the house of a murdered woman weighed the odds even more heavily against her.

That evening, Detective Superintendent Pass visited

the Calverts. Louie shuffled to the door wearing Lily's boots and a headscarf she had snatched from her during that final struggle. Blunder number two.

The suitcase was still in the living-room and when questioned Louie again claimed that it contained clothes for the baby. The superintendent lifted it and shook his head. "It's much too heavy for that," he said. "We'll have to open it."

Once opened, the case revealed cutlery, crockery and linen. . . the same missing items over which Lily had originally gone to the police. Blunder number three.

Louie was arrested, taken to a police station and charged with murder. "It's a lie. I didn't do it," she screamed. "I reserve my defence until the trial."

Later a badly shaken Arthur Calvert was told the whole story of how his wife had obtained the baby and then committed murder to avoid facing a theft charge over a few items that were almost worthless.

Louie appeared before Mr. Justice Wright and the trial proved to be a mere formality. The Crown produced twenty-five witnesses; but Louie's counsel, Dr E.C. Chappell, couldn't find a single person prepared to come forward and speak on her behalf.

The jury returned the expected guilty verdict and she was asked by the clerk of the court whether she had anything to say before the sentence was announced.

"Yes, sir," replied Louie, "I'm pregnant."

There was uproar in court. Louie was taken down to the cells; and Doctor Hoyland-Smith and a nurse were sent to examine her. Some twenty minutes later, Louie was ushered back into the dock and the doctor, looking very worried, stepped into the witness box.

The judge asked, "Are you able to confirm to the court that the prisoner is indeed pregnant?"

The doctor shook his head. "I fear, my Lord, I can't," he said. "I can find nothing to suggest pregnancy." He paused. "At least, not at this stage."

The judge donned the black cap and, as the sentence of death was passed, two members of the jury fainted.

Louie attended her appeal in London and listened as the Lord Chief Justice dismissed it, saying, "It's entirely possible that she went to the house of the dead woman simply to steal. But we have to be influenced by the fact that she declined to give evidence at her trial. So we have no grounds for overturning the verdict reached that day."

As the day of her execution approached, she made a last dramatic attempt to delay the inevitable. She confessed to prison officers that, before becoming Arthur Calvert's housekeeper, she had murdered a man called John William Frobisher whose body had been found floating in a Leeds canal.

However the Home Secretary, Sir William Joynson-Hicks, refused to interfere with the sentence and Louie Calvert was hanged on June 26, 1926, at Strangeways Prison.

On this occasion, at least, it seems likely that she was telling the truth. Frobisher's body had been identified by his housekeeper, Louisa Jackson, and an open verdict of 'found drowned' was recorded. . . despite much disquiet on the part of the police.

Louisa Jackson's real name was Louie Gomersall, later Louie Calvert!

# 14

# THE HANGING JUDGE

*"I will deliver myself to you, and I will go to
the police station. I must have been mad."
James Richardson, speaking to his employer
Francis Chamberlain.*

Mr. Justice Mathew rolled up the sleeves of his gown as
though to physically chastise the poor wretch weeping in
the dock. His face was stern and his eyes burned with
zealot's fire.

"How does he plead?" he asked. "I couldn't hear."

"Not guilty, my Lord," replied the clerk of the court.

"Not guilty!" echoed the judge, as though he could
scarcely credit the evidence of his own ears. He gave a
massive shrug for the benefit of the jury. Then, turning
the full force of his personality upon the prisoner, he
thundered, "In my court, I expect your replies to be loud
and clear. I can't abide mumbling. Do you understand?"

"Yes, sir," replied the prisoner humbly.

"Yes, my Lord," corrected the judge. "Remember
that."

Even in the British courts of a century ago, Mr. Justice
Mathew was regarded as a terrifying judge. Defence
counsels, let alone prisoners, would shudder when told
that he would be presiding over their case. He was known
as 'The Hanging Judge' and with good reason.

He believed it was his duty to make sure that all those who appeared before him charged with murder should soon be dangling at the end of a rope. It wasn't that he was necessarily a bad man or even a cruel one. He just had a different view of his role to that of most of his fellow judges. He had much in common with the fire and brimstone preacher. A deeply religious man, he believed that it was his duty to purge the world of sin, and consequently of sinners. He further believed that the police would never have charged a man with murder unless they were first sure of his guilt. . . and so it was his task to convince the jury of this obvious truth.

He was having a good week. Three times, in the space of so many days, he had donned the black cap and pronounced the sentence of death. The latest had been this very morning. . . and now, if he had his way, this wretch before him would be lodged in the condemned cell by nightfall.

The 'wretch' in question was actually a rather pleasant-looking man of twenty-three named James Richardson who until recently had led a totally blameless life. He was hard-working, polite, friendly and immensely popular with his workmates at the brick and carbon plant in Barnsley owned by the local tycoons, Humphrey and Francis Chamberlain.

And then on a cold day in March, 1880, his whole world fell apart. He had arrived for work at twenty to seven, twenty minutes before his starting time. During the five years he'd been at the plant, he'd never once been late, never once been in trouble.

And so his workmates were surprised to see Richardson engaged in a series of angry conversations with the foreman, William Berridge, during the first hour of the day. Berridge was a hard taskmaster who took a certain pride in his reputation for ruthlessness. He was fond of saying, "I never believe in giving a man a second chance. One mistake and they're out." Yet even Berridge had hitherto been unable to find fault with Richardson. The rest of the work force could only guess at the cause of the argument, because the roar of the machinery blotted out the words. Just after eight o'clock, another row broke out between the two men and the normally mild-tempered Richardson threw the brush he'd been holding at the foreman and stormed off.

He wasn't seen at the works again until eleven-thirty, when he knocked on the door of the office. The door was opened by the clerk, a young boy called Illingworth. He invited Richardson into the outer room, but Richardson declined the offer when he spotted Berridge standing in the inner sanctum, talking to the boss, Francis Chamberlain.

Illingworth later recounted that Richardson appeared to be very nervous and agitated; and paced up and down outside the office, clearly waiting for Berridge and Chamberlain to finish their conversation.

When Berridge finally emerged, he spotted Richardson and moved towards him menacingly as though about to resume the argument. But before he could utter a word, Richardson drew a gun from his pocket and shot the foreman three times.

He then ran across the yard chased by Francis Chamberlain. But they hadn't gone far before Richardson stopped, turned and said, "I will deliver myself to you, and I will go to the police station. I must have been mad."

He handed the gun butt first to his boss and said, "You've been a good employer and I didn't mean to cause you trouble. I'm sorry about that."

Berridge was taken to hospital, where he survived for a week before dying from a head wound.

On Thursday, May 3, 1888, Richardson was led weeping into the dock before Mr. Justice Mathew and, after a great effort, pleaded not guilty. But he seemed so overwhelmed by the enormity of his crime and the forbidding presence of the judge that he made little or no effort to defend himself.

His defence counsel, Mr. Mellor, nevertheless made a passionate speech on his behalf, despite frequent interruptions from the judge. He pointed out that

Richardson had led a blameless life and that he had been popular with workmates and employers alike. He reminded the jury that his boss, Francis Chamberlain, had been quick to speak up on his behalf.

Then turning to the character of Berridge, he described him as a tyrant and a bully, a man who enjoyed exercising his power in cruel ways. On that fateful day, he had fired Richardson on little more than a whim. He had chosen to ignore the fact that for five years Richardson had held a perfect record, never late for work, and without a single bad mark against him.

"It was the injustice of this act," claimed Mr. Mellor, "that drove the prisoner to commit this act so out of character. When he said to his employer 'I must have been mad' that was surely the literal truth. For that brief spell of time, he was mad. . . driven that way by another man's cruelty."

However the judge summed up heavily on the side of the prosecution and the jury found him guilty of wilful murder and failed to add any recommendation for mercy.

Most judges when sentencing a man to death tended to get the matter over as swiftly and as painlessly as possible, but not Mr. Justice Mathew. He chose instead to deliver a homily, in the midst of which he said, "You have sent a man who appeared to be inoffensive to the next world. Now you must prepare to follow him."

The citizens of Barnsley, Richardson's home town, bombarded the Home Secretary with petitions for his reprieve. Even the Queen was approached, but all to no avail. On May 22, Richardson walked firmly to the gallows, where he was hanged by James Billington.

He was the only one of the four men sentenced to death that week by Mr. Justice Mathew who paid the ultimate price. The other three were reprieved, due to flaws in the judge's summing up.

Upon learning this, Mr. Justice Mathew was said to be "mortified".

# 15

# THE BEST MATE

*"So, you were very quiet, peaceable poachers.*
*Is that a fair description?"*
*Counsel's question to a witness.*

It was one of those nights when the sky comes down and
wraps itself around the world. The clouds squatted on the
rooftops of Rotherham and yet the rain refused to fall.
The wind too had gone away, leaving an eerie silence in
its wake.

On such nights, mild little wives have been known to
finger rolling-pins and study their loved ones with a
calculating eye. And even the most well-meaning men
have felt the hair rising along the napes of their necks.

Yet Sam Barker and his friends seemed singularly
unaffected by the coming storm. They walked along the
street, laughing and joking, without a care in the world.
The mood didn't change as Arthur Jeffries stepped out of
a nearby passageway.

"Good night, Arthur," said Barker.

"Good night to you, you bugger," replied Jeffries.

Barker laughed and said, "Bugger you too, Arthur,"
and was about to walk on when Jeffries suddenly punched
him on the chin.

He then grabbed hold of Barker's collar and the two
men disappeared into the dark passageway, still clinging
to one another.

The others stood listening to the sounds of scuffling, until the two fighters emerged on to the street again. Then Barker tumbled to the ground, bleeding profusely from the chest. He lay ominously still. Having heard the sounds of combat, Mrs. Jeffries came running and fell over Barker's body.

She took one look and screamed at her husband, "Now tha's done it!" She then hurried him home and locked the door.

The remaining men picked up their friend and carried him to one of the nearby houses. A doctor was called, but all he could do was pronounce Barker dead.

Jeffries was arrested and when told that Barker was dead, he said, "I hope not. I won't believe it."

His home and the passageway weren't searched until the following morning and by then the murder weapon had disappeared, never to be found.

The sad irony behind the crime was that Sam Barker had been Arthur Jeffries' best mate for nearly thirty years; and during that time they'd been almost inseparable. They had been members of a poaching gang that operated around the South Yorkshire town of Rotherham. By day the gang, some six in number, all worked as colliers; by night, they poached the local land to supplement their meagre wages.

But in October, 1904, some disagreement had arisen between Jeffries and the other members of the gang and since then they had gone poaching without him. He resented this greatly and had been heard to threaten various members with a knife or a sharpened blacksmith's file.

Then on the night of Saturday, November 12, that threat became reality. Jeffries was charged and appeared before Mr. Justice Grantham, a stroke of bad luck for a poacher, especially one charged with murder. Sir William Grantham was a country squire with a big estate and consequently no admirer of poachers.

The Crown was represented by Mr.T.R. Wright and

Mr. Ball, while Mr. Trotter conducted the defence. Considering that this was a murder trial, the proceedings were remarkably light-hearted.

George Houldon, a collier, stated that he had known Barker for some years, and the prisoner for about two years. On one occasion, he remembered the prisoner saying, "He would reighton with one of us before long."

The Judge: "What does that mean in your dialect?"

The Witness: "That he would do us some harm."

Mr. Trotter: "Did he not say he would reighton up with one of you?"

The Witness: "Yes, it's just the same thing. He had threatened to 'do' for one of us."

Houldon went on to say that he had never heard any other member of the gang threaten anybody.

Mr. Trotter: "So, you were very quiet, peaceable poachers. Is that a fair description?"

The Witness: "Yes, sir." This answer was met with gales of laughter from the court with the judge likewise much amused.

Joseph Beal, another collier, said he had known the prisoner for some five or six years.

Mr. Trotter: "Were you a member of this poaching gang?"

The Witness: "I was, sir." (Laughter)

Mr. Trotter: "The gang were very quiet, peaceable men?"

The Witness. "Yes."

Mr. Trotter: "And Barker was quiet and peaceable?"

The Witness: "As harmless as a lamb." (Laughter)

Mr. Trotter: "And you were as quiet and harmless as a lamb?"

The Witness: "In that respect I was, sir."

Other witnesses said that after Jeffries had sworn at the group, they heard him say something like, "Oh, take that." Then Barker had fallen to the ground; but no one recalled seeing a knife or any other weapon.

A doctor said that a sharp instrument, possibly a thin

knife or a file, had penetrated the aorta.

Arthur Jeffries had declined to give evidence on his own behalf; and appeared to be genuinely stricken by the death of his long-time friend.

Mr. Trotter asked the jury to consider whether there were circumstances connected with the fight which would entitle them to say that this wasn't murder but simply the outcome of a struggle which would reduce the offence to manslaughter.

During his summing up, the judge heavily criticised the police for failing to search the passageway or the prisoner's house until the following morning. By which time, the lethal weapon had conveniently disappeared.

After an absence of thirty-seven minutes, the jury found Jeffries guilty of murder; but added a strong recommendation for mercy. In passing sentence, the judge said that the verdict was the only one which met the justice of the case.

Arthur Jeffries, aged forty-four, was hanged on December 29, 1904. John Billington was the executioner, assisted by Henry Pierrepoint.

It had been a sad and a strange end to a friendship.

# 16

# THE INNOCENTEST MAN

*"It was only a little revolver."*
*Patrick Morley, addressing the judge.*

Patrick Morley surveyed his wife Elizabeth across the breakfast table with sudden interest. "Who gave you that shiner?" he asked.

Elizabeth, a slim, dispirited woman, shrugged and didn't answer.

Morley chewed his bacon thoughtfully. "Just give me his name and I'll go see him."

Elizabeth sighed and uttered not a word.

Morley gulped down his tea. "Don't go silent on me," he said. "Just tell me and I'll sort him out for you. No one, but no one, touches my woman. Do you hear me?"

She looked at him for the first time. "You daft bugger," she said, "you gave me that shiner when you came in last night. You were the one who blacked my eye. Nobody else did."

He was genuinely astonished. "Are you sure?" he asked.

"Of course I'm sure," she said.

"But what was the reason, what had you done to deserve that?"

"You know you never need a reason when you've drink taken," she replied. "Once you're drunk, you'll hit anything that moves."

He pondered over this for a while and then he nodded slowly, because he knew this was true. "I'm sorry, luv," he said. "I really am. It won't happen again."

But they both knew it would; for Pat Morley had very little control over his own wild nature. He was in many ways the caricature of the music hall Irishman. He was a labourer with the strength of three normal men and the mind of a small boy.

He was the butt of a thousand jokes and he fell for them all. He had once been told the story about the Irishman who had set out to swim the Channel. At the halfway point, he had decided he was too tired to reach the French coast; so he'd turned round and swum back to England.

Morley had followed this with some interest. Then after some thought, he asked, "Did he make it all right?"

"Oh, yes," said the teller of the tale, "he was still as strong as a lion."

"That's good," said Morley. He didn't see anything odd in that story.

Even when he realised that his leg was being pulled, he took it all in great good humour. . . that is when he was sober. When he'd been drinking, he was a very different proposition; and other men stepped very quietly around him.

The unfortunate Elizabeth bore the brunt of his violence. Twice she went to the police and twice he was bound over to keep the peace. On the second occasion, he was searched and the police found a revolver in his pocket. This was confiscated. The nights of violence were followed by mornings of contrition. But finally after one beating too many, his wife packed her belongings and moved into lodgings in Batley.

Full of remorse, Morley asked her to come home with him. He promised that he would never lift a hand against her again; but she had heard that too many times before. So she refused and Morley, running true to form, set out to drown his sorrows.

On Saturday, September 21, he hatched a drunken plot. He bought another revolver and went to visit his wife once more. He found her in the kitchen of her apartment with a young girl called Lucy Cooper. They talked for a few minutes and then he said, "Elizabeth, lend me a shilling."

She explained that she was on piece-work at the local factory and consequently hadn't any money.

Immediately he heard this, he said, "Get out, Elizabeth."

So saying, he drew the revolver from his pocket and shot her. She fell to the ground and died almost instantly. He then turned the gun on himself, but (music-hall Irishman to the end) he missed. His hand was shaking so badly that the bullet flew over his shoulder and buried itself in the wall.

By now Lucy Cooper was running around the kitchen, shouting, "Murder! murder!"

Her screams attracted the attention of a neighbour called Fred Ashton who came in and disarmed Morley who made no attempt to resist. He was suddenly sober and shocked. The police and a doctor were called. And when Morley was told that his wife was dead, he said, "I'm very sorry. I hope her soul is in Heaven."

At the police station, he made a voluntary statement in the presence of Sergeant Machell. In this, he said, "I've been begging my wife to leave the lodgings, to come with me and get a house. If she had done this, I was going to throw the revolver away where it would never be found. But she refused. We walked around the town together and I continually begged her to change her mind and she continually refused. I knew that if she didn't change her mind, she would have to die for it; and I would have given her anything if only she could have said, 'Yes', but she couldn't be persuaded. So tonight I went to see her again. I asked her to lend me a shilling. If she had given me a shilling, I would have gone away. I wouldn't have shot her."

He was charged and appeared before Mr. Justice Grantham. Mr. Harold Thomas led for the Crown; and at the request of the judge, Mr. A. Bromet undertook the defence of the prisoner.

When the charge was read out to him, Morley replied, "Not guilty. I don't remember." And that remark set the pattern for the trial. No prisoner ever looked more confused.

For the defence, Mr. Bromet called Thomas Morley, the prisoner's brother, who declared, "Pat hasn't been 'right square' in his head for ten years and he's been getting worse since his marriage."

He added that they had two cousins in Irish asylums and that another brother Michael "hasn't been right in the head since the day he was born." There were also two aunts who "weren't quite right."

Mr. Bromet suggested that Morley hadn't really meant to shoot his wife, that he only wanted to frighten her; so that she would return to him.

"If he had actually aimed at her," he said, "he would have missed. . . the same way as he did when he aimed at himself. He is not a very good shot."

At this, a smile flickered across the face of the judge. But in his summing up, he observed that if the evidence was to be believed the deed had been done intentionally and not by accident.

The jury found Pat Morley guilty. Asked whether he had anything to say before being sentenced, the prisoner made a long rambling speech in which he addressed the judge variously as 'yur riverence' and 'yur lordliness'.

He said, "I was more fit to be in an asylum than at large on the night when I shot my wife. I have a weak head and a weak chest and I told the doctors that. So I hope you'll give me a chance, because I hadn't intended to shoot the woman, only to frighten her. I had been sober for twelve months; but after Elizabeth moved out, I took to the drink again."

He paused as though the speech was finished, but then

continued, saying, "You see, yur riverence, it was only a little revolver. I hadn't thought the trigger would go off."

He paused again and the judge asked him whether this was indeed the end.

"Almost, yur lordliness," replied Morley, "almost. But I just want to say that although I done it, I'm the innocentest man in the world. I also want you to know that I have a testimonial from Ireland where I was brought up. I also have as good a character as any man in the world."

The judge mercifully made no comment on this. He merely pointed out that drink could be no excuse for a crime such as this, and sentenced him to death. Morley, who seemed unable to grasp the seriousness of the situation, was led to the cells. He was executed by James Billington on December 31, 1895. New Year's Eve. A strange day on which to die.

# 17
# THE PEACEMAKER

*"Send your folks, please. I have killed my wife and
child." Lock Ah Tam's phone call to the police.*

Lock Ah Tam was a cool man. Storms and tempests and
guns on the streets of the city were old hat to him. He was
the kind who would have greeted the end of the world with
a shrug and another Scotch tipped down the hatch.

You needed to be a bit like that if you were to be a boss
on Liverpool's tough waterfront during the early nineteen
hundreds. He headed the European branch of the Jack Ah
Tia, an organisation of Chinese stevedores with headquarters in Hong Kong. He founded the Chinese Progress
Club where sailors from the Orient could find a home
from home. And he had also been appointed as the
superintendent of Chinese sailors for three British
steamship companies.

They called him 'The Peacemaker', because it was said
that he was the only man capable of controlling the warlike
factions on the docks. His attributes were two-fold . . . a
pair of iron hands which he could use with deadly effect
whenever the need arose, coupled with a good nature. It
was a common sight to see him pull two fighting seamen
apart and then lecture them with the broadest of smiles, as
though it had all been a joke. Inevitably the two com-
batants would soon be smiling too.

He was equally good natured in his private life, a loving

husband to his Welsh-born wife Catherine and a soft touch of a dad to his son Lock Ling and his two daughters, Doris and Cecilia.

Then one night in February, 1918, Tam was having a drink with friends in the Progress Club when the door was broken down by a gang of drunken Russian sailors. A smiling Tam seized two of the invaders with those iron hands and was just about to preach the message of peace when another struck him over the head with the weighted end of a snooker cue. He went down as though poleaxed. The Russians were vanquished and thrown out into the night, but Tam still remained unconscious on the floor.

His friends revived him and after gingerly feeling the bump on his head, the smile returned. He listened for a while to the sailors' talk of a revenge raid upon the Russians, then held up his hand commanding silence. "They were just drunk, that's all," he said. "They didn't mean any real harm. Just leave everything to me. I'll talk to them in the morning when they're sober. They'll apologise and pay for the damage like the good fellows they really are. Believe me, that's the best way."

The sailors were just about to applaud this statesmanlike speech when an amazing change came over Tam. His eyes began to bulge from their sockets and saliva frothed from his mouth. He seized a snooker cue and smashed the bottles behind the bar. Then he snapped the cue in two, as though it was little more than a matchstick and hurled the two ends through the window. Just as suddenly as it had come, the mood went away. He smiled. "Just leave it to me," he said. "I'll talk to them."

But these dramatic changes of mood continued. He would be quiet and peaceful one moment, then uncontrollably violent the next. He began drinking heavily and at such times men walked in fear of him. The same pattern was followed at home. Most of the time, he would be a loving husband and caring dad; and then suddenly he would become a monster. He would roar like a bull, stamp his feet and break crockery; but to his credit, he never physically harmed his family.

Yet in his saner moments, he had this fear that one day he might. His son Lock Ling was the apple of his eye and yet they were beginning to have some terrible arguments. So Tam, very much aware of his own dark nature, sent his much-loved son to college in China, for his own safety.

Tam's wisdom, which had been almost legendary on the waterfront, had deserted him. His business ventures began to suffer. One crippling loss in 1924 cost him £10,000 and landed him in the bankruptcy court.

In November, 1925, Lock Ling returned home, college completed, and was welcomed like the prodigal son. A delighted Tam decided to throw a party to celebrate his son's coming of age. A selected group of family and friends came to the house and Tam was his old warm and genial self. The party was a great success and the last guest left just after midnight.

Then in the early hours of the following morning, P.C. Drysdale was sitting at his desk in the Birkenhead Central police station when his phone rang and a confused, foreign-sounding voice said, "Tam. . . shot. . . kill wife and child."

"Who is that speaking?" Drysdale asked.

"Lock Ah Tam, send your folks, please. I have killed my wife and child. My house is 122 Prince Street."

When the police arrived at the house, they were faced by an awful scene. Catherine and her youngest daughter Cecilia, aged eighteen, lay dead, killed by gunshots. Tam's other daughter Doris, aged twenty, lay fatally wounded.

Tam himself appeared quite calm and sat in an armchair smoking a cigarette. As the police led him away, he turned to his friend and neighbour Kwok Tsan Chin and said, "I'm in trouble. You will look after the business; do your best. If I am hung, get my body out and bury me by my wife."

At the police station, Tam's demeanour altered drastically. He became so wild and excited, with his eyes bulging and mouth frothing, that the superintendent refused to charge him. Later, when charged, he was asked whether he had anything to say.

He replied, "Nothing at present, nothing at present, nothing at the present time."

Chinese from all over Britain contributed to a defence fund; and none other than the distinguished Sir Edward Marshall Hall was briefed to lead Tam's defence at the forthcoming Chester Assizes. Sir Ellis Griffiths prosecuted and the judge was Mr. Justice Mackinnon, who was presiding over his first murder trial.

Tam pleaded not guilty to the three charges of murder on the indictment. But Sir Edward realised that he had a mammoth task to secure any other verdict than that of 'guilty of murder.'

He felt that there could be only one possible defence — namely that Tam had committed the murders while in a state of "unconscious automatism" brought about by an epileptic fit. Sir Edward suggested that the blow to the head inflicted by the Russian sailor had affected his brain and made him epileptic. The epilepsy brought on a desire for alcohol which in turn intensified the fits. Also the worry of the bankruptcy had caused a further disturbance to his already overwrought mind.

Unfortunately for Tam, the plea of insanity had to satisfy the rigid test of the McNaghten rules. The judge pointed out to the jury, somewhat reluctantly it seemed, that Tam had phoned the police immediately after killing his wife and daughters; and that this showed that he fully appreciated the nature of the act. Moreover it showed that he was aware of the fact that what he had done was wrong.

This must have been in the forefront of their minds when, after a retirement of only twelve minutes, they returned a verdict of guilty.

The black cap was placed on the judge's head and, with tears running down his cheeks, he passed the sentence of death.

Lock Ah Tam, however, remained calm and accepted his fate with an air of indifference which he maintained up to the moment of his execution on March 23, 1926.

In his death cell, his good nature had returned. He was once more The Peacemaker.

# 18

# DEATH OF A NURSE

*"My wife is lying dead on the river bank."*
*Bert Salisbury speaking to Police Sergeant King.*

Bert Salisbury watched her walking down the ward. The uniform, white and freshly starched, rustled a little and gave only a frustrating hint of the well-rounded figure beneath. He had always had a thing about nurses and this one fitted very neatly into his wildest fantasies. He was already imagining what the top of her thighs would look like above the black stockings. He was quite sure they would be white.

It had been a long time since Bert had seen a woman, let alone talked to one. For this was September, 1918, and he had just been shipped home from France, suffering from shrapnel wounds and trench fever. But lying in bed watching the nurse walk on by he felt wonderful. He knew her name was Alice and he was just wondering how he could get to know her better when she stopped beside his bed.

"Hello," she said with a smile, "and how are you feeling today?"

He shrugged, "Pretty miserable until now, but just the sight of you has cheered me up."

She was quite used to being chatted up by the never-ending line of wounded soldiers who came to the hospital, and she really didn't mind. She looked upon them all as heroes and rather enjoyed the flattery. Her own husband, Mark Pearson, was in France too. . . and she missed him in every way.

She looked at his chart. "Well, your temperature's coming down nicely," she said. "I think you'll survive."

She checked his pulse, holding his wrist gently. He moved his other hand to cover hers. She thought for a moment of pushing it away and then changed her mind. He really wasn't doing any harm; and anyway, after all he'd been through for King and country, he deserved a little comfort.

"Will you come back and see me later?" he asked.

"How about my other patients?"

He smiled and when he smiled he looked quite handsome. "I'm sure they can spare you," he said. And then he added cleverly, "It will help me get better. I'm very lonely."

It touched a chord in her being; for despite all the hustle and bustle of hospital life, she was lonely too. "All right, tonight when I come off duty, just for a few moments," she promised. Her eyes twinkled. "Don't go away," she said.

So began a friendship between nurse and patient that had to be played low key. Hospital managements scarcely encourage this sort of thing.

By the time Bert Salisbury was finally discharged, the war was over. Alice took a fortnight's leave and they went away together on holiday. They started out as friends and almost inevitably became lovers.

Her husband Mark Pearson returned home in the spring of 1919 to find a 'Dear John' letter waiting for him. Alice was desperately sorry, but she had fallen madly in love with another man and wouldn't be coming back. She hoped that he would understand and find it in his heart to forgive her.

He divorced her, naming Salisbury as co-respondent. A decree nisi was granted in the summer of that same year.

David Lloyd George, the Prime Minister of the day, had promised the troops that they would return to a 'Land Fit For Heroes', but the reality was rather different. The country was in the grip of depression and jobs were hard to find. Bert Salisbury joined the ranks of the unemployed; and they were both discovering that love on the dole is not all that it's cracked up to be. Alice had a few hundred pounds of her own and this enabled them to live as husband and wife in lodgings at Southport. They were described by their landlady as being "sober, quiet and respectable." But their money was running out fast and the future looked bleak.

On Sunday, March 21, 1920, they left their lodgings together soon after lunch. At 6.30 p.m., they were seen near the Royal Hotel in Formby, heading in the direction of Liverpool. Just after half-past seven, Salisbury (who was now alone) went into the Blundell Arms and had a whisky and soda. He had an argument with the barman whom he accused of staring at him. A dock labourer called Clayton was standing at the bar, listening to the argument; and he noticed that Salisbury kept taking a revolver out of his pocket and putting it back again.

Salisbury left the pub at closing time and promptly fell flat on his face. Clayton picked him up and, taking him to a street lamp, told him to wipe his nose which was bleeding. Salisbury suddenly pulled out the revolver and said, "I have just put four bullets into my wife."

Clayton took the revolver away from Salisbury and dragged him by the scruff of the neck to the nearest police station, where he was taken into custody on a charge of drunkenness. There were five live cartridges in the gun which Clayton handed to Inspector Kenyon, but Clayton failed to inform the police about the remark Salisbury had made moments earlier – namely, "I have just put four bullets into my wife."

Salisbury refused to speak even to the police and he was described as being "rather drunk and rather silly." He was searched and they found in his possession thirty-six live cartridges which fitted the revolver, a lady's gold watch, gold guard and locket. He was then put in a cell to sleep it off.

At seven o'clock the following morning, Police Sergeant King went to the cell with the intention of getting the prisoner's name and address. Salisbury gave his name, but refused to give an address.

The sergeant asked, "Where does your wife live?"

Salisbury shrugged. "My wife is lying dead on the river bank past Tommy Rimmer's on the main road. I shot her last night."

Sergeant King had the area searched and sure enough at the foot of the embankment of the River Alt, about a mile from the Blundell Arms, they found the body of Alice Pearson. Her face was covered with blood and there were four wounds on the temple. Two bullets were later removed from the brain.

On Thursday, April 22, 1920, Salisbury stepped into the dock at the Liverpool Assizes, wearing a grey suit and looking every inch a soldier as he stood to attention. The charge was read out to him and he answered, "Guilty."

A moment of silence followed, then Mr. Justice M'Cardie said, "In this case, I shall direct that a plea of 'Not Guilty' be entered. I deem it desirable, when a charge of murder is made, that the case should be established against the person charged in open court so that all the facts connected with the crime may be considered. The prisoner has the advantage of being represented by Mr. Madden."

Mr. A.J. Ashton outlined the prosecution's case, telling the jury that Salisbury had gone to America some twenty years earlier and then returned to England on the outbreak of war to fight for King and country. The evidence for the Crown was completed in less than two hours.

The defence didn't call any witnesses, but Mr. Madden claimed that his client was of unsound mind four days after the murder had been committed and that there could be no doubt of that.

The delirium tremens from which he was then suffering must have been due to his heavy drinking before the time of the tragedy. There must have been implanted in him already the seeds of that disease. And that being so, he couldn't have known what he was doing when he shot Alice.

The prisoner, said Mr. Madden, had been prevented by the law from putting the rope around his own neck. Subject to the direction from the judge, he suggested that it would be open to the jury to return a manslaughter verdict. But Mr. Madden submitted the much finer issue that the prisoner was insane at the time of the tragedy, and therefore not responsible for his actions.

The judge said he couldn't see how the question of manslaughter could apply in this case; because whoever fired the shots must have fired with the intention to kill. The question for the jury was whether the verdict should be wilful murder or guilty but insane.

The jury retired for twenty minutes and then returned a verdict of wilful murder. Salisbury, still the soldier standing to attention, was asked whether he had anything to say before being sentenced.

He replied politely, "No thank you, sir," and appeared totally unmoved as the black cap was placed on the judge's head.

Bert Salisbury was hanged alongside William Waddington, who had been convicted of the murder of a seven-year-old girl at Oldham. The date was May 11 and John Ellis, a barber, was the executioner.

From the moment of the shooting, Salisbury had seemingly resigned himself to his own death. He made no attempt to confide in anyone. So why he killed the woman he loved must remain for ever a mystery. And it must be deemed possible that the man who squeezed the trigger didn't know either.

# 19

# THUNDER-THIGHS

*"We were the kind of people who could
neither live with each other, nor live without
each other." Dr. Buck Ruxton, in the witness box,
speaking about his wife Isabella.*

"Isabella, pull your dress down," said Dr Buck Ruxton. "Everyone's looking at your legs."

"Perhaps that's because they like looking at them," replied his wife Isabella, making no attempt to lower the hem. And then turning to their companion Charlie Pugh, she asked artfully, "Do you like looking at my legs, Charlie?"

It was early evening and yet Charlie was already a little drunk and seemingly unaware of his own wife's hand upon his sleeve. "Of course, I do," he replied dutifully. "We all do. They're the raunchiest legs in town. You ought to be proud to have a wife with legs such as that, Buck."

Ruxton, a notoriously jealous man, was too angry to reply.

In fact, the legs of Isabella were an oddity. The thighs were well rounded and, as an admirer once wrote, formidable. But that plumpness continued all the way down to the ankle. If you were a connoisseur of the classic leg, then Isabella was not the lady for you. But on the other hand if you liked your women soft to touch, you might well have found the legs of Isabella decidedly erotic. In Lancaster, they had earnt her the nickname of 'Thunder-thighs'.

Certainly she wasn't adverse to flashing them around a little. She was both a tease and a flirt. . . and the more jealous her husband became, the more she would tease and flirt. And so it was in the restaurant that night. Soon after they'd been seated at their table, she slipped off her shoes and began to play her own version of footsie, tickling Charlie's shin with her toes and then moving slowly ever upwards.

At first, there was no outward sign. Charlie chatted to his wife as though nothing untoward was happening beneath the tablecloth. Buck Ruxton knew just the same. Isabella had played this game before with other men. Eventually her stockinged foot began to inch its way along Charlie's inner thigh. He bore this stoically as long as he could and then finally in retaliation, he grabbed her ankle and began to tickle the sole of her foot. At which point, they both collapsed into laughter. Ruxton was so angry that he didn't utter another word during the entire course of the meal.

This silence persisted on the journey home; and it was only when they'd entered their own house that the doctor allowed his full fury to erupt.

"You whore," he shouted, "you make yourself look cheap and you make me look cheap too. How many times have you slept with him?"

She was laughing, pretending to count her fingers. Then shaking her head, she said, "I can't really remember. I'll have to ask Charlie next time I see him."

She had misjudged his anger. He suddenly slapped her hard across the face. He raised his right fist, held it aloft for what seemed an eternity and slowly lowered it. He was shaking as though from a fever. "One of these days," he said, "I'll finish you. Do you hear me? I'll finish you."

"You poor damn fool," said Isabella quietly and a little sadly. "Don't you know I'm only teasing you?"

So saying, she stepped into his arms and kissed him. This kiss began with tenderness and ended in passion. Five minutes later, they were making love on the hearthrug as though there were no tomorrows.

Their love making was always at its best on nights such as this. First she would tease and torment him, fan the fires of his jealousy. Then they would have a row, kiss and make up.

Isabella confided to her friends that on normal occasions, Ruxton was a pussycat of a lover; but once roused by jealousy, he could be a veritable tiger in bed. It was something that only a psychiatrist could hope to understand. It was also a dangerous game for Isabella to play. Twice she had to call in the police for protection and on another occasion she had left home for several months.

It was really a case of 'physician heal thyself' for there was never any evidence to suggest that Isabella had been unfaithful. Yet Ruxton continued to believe that she was sleeping with just about every man she met.

If she had been a wiser lady, she wouldn't have deliberately encouraged that jealousy with her flirting and teasing. But the intention was understandable. She wanted their love making to be passionate; and without the anger, it was apparently joyless.

She was, to be precise, his common-law wife and her real name was Isabella Van Ess. Ruxton's real name was Bukhtyar Rustomji Ratanji Hakim, but he preferred the more English sounding version. In 1928, Ruxton and Isabella decided to live together; and when their eldest child Elizabeth was born, Isabella took Ruxton's name.

For seven years, they stayed together and Isabella played her dangerous game; and then on September 14, 1935, her luck finally ran out. On that day, she set off alone in the family car to meet her sisters in Blackpool. They viewed the famous illuminations together and then shortly before midnight, she left her sisters and drove away. . . never to be seen alive again.

The following day, the Ruxtons' charlady received a

visit from Ruxton. He told Mrs. Agnes Oxley not to bother coming in today, because Mrs. Ruxton and Mary Rogerson (nanny to the Ruxtons' three children) had gone on holiday to Edinburgh. "Come in as usual tomorrow," he added.

Later that morning, he took the children to a friend's house, asking her to look after them while his wife was away. The lady noticed that Ruxton's right hand was swathed in bandages. He explained that he had cut his hand while opening a tin-can. The real reason for the cut was soon to become all too clear and to remain etched in the woman's memory for the rest of her life.

On that same Sunday afternoon, he asked another woman to scrub his staircase and landing so that the decorators could start work. She noticed that the bath was stained a peculiar yellow colour; and that no matter how hard she scrubbed, the stain remained. She also attempted to clean a carpet; and when she poured water on it, the residue came off coloured bright red.

Two weeks later, a Miss Susan Johnson was walking across a bridge spanning the Gardenholme Linn, a tributary of the River Annan. She looked into the gully below and spotted what she thought to be a human arm. She told her brother and he went to look for himself. He found the arm and several packages containing human remains. The grisly task of collecting the packages was left to the Dumfriesshire police, who conveyed the remains to a mortuary at Moffat.

It was discovered that the remains had come from two bodies, both female. One, it was decided, was young. . . the other middle-aged. The pieces of flesh and internal organs were wrapped in female clothing with an outer covering of newspaper.

The first piece in the jigsaw came from the sheets of newspaper. Wrapped around one parcel were sheets from the *Sunday Graphic*. This particular slip edition had only been released in Lancaster and Morecombe. The date on the paper was September 15, 1935.

The next piece of the jigsaw was spotted by a policeman reading a story in the *Glasgow Daily Record*. It told of the disappearance of a young woman from Lancaster called Mary Rogerson, nanny to a respectable doctor. She had disappeared in September. Investigations revealed that the doctor was called Buck Ruxton and that coincidentally Mrs. Ruxton had vanished at the same time.

A distressed Mrs. Jessie Rogerson, stepmother of Mary, was driven to the mortuary to see if she could identify the clothing used to wrap the grisly remains. Sadly for Mrs. Rogerson, she immediately recognised a blouse she had given to Mary after repairing it with a distinctive patch.

Now that a connection between the dismembered bodies and the Ruxton family had been established, the Lancaster police took over the investigations, headed by the Chief Constable, Captain Henry Vann.

Ruxton had already visited the Chief Constable to ask for his help in stopping the rumours and the gossip which were already linking him with the discovery at Moffat.

At the time, it had suited the police to take the pressure off Ruxton. So they issued a statement to the newspapers, which seemed to satisfy the doctor.

But on October 13, Ruxton was arrested and charged with the murder of Mary Rogerson; and on November 5, he was further charged with the murder of Isabella.

His reply: "That's absolute bunkum, with a capital B."

He was tried for the murder of Isabella only and he pleaded not guilty. Counsel for the Crown were Mr. J.C. Jackson, Mr. Maxwell Fyfe and Mr. Hartley Shawcross. Mr. Norman Birkett and Mr. Philip Kershaw defended. Mr. Justice (later Lord Justice) Singleton presided.

The Crown's case rested mainly with their three pathologists, Professor John Glaister, Professor of Forensic Medicine at Glasgow University; Professor James C. Brash, Professor of Anatomy at Edinburgh University; and perhaps the most famous member of the trio, Professor (later Sir) Sydney Smith, Professor of Forensic Medicine at Edinburgh University.

The two bodies were reconstructed by the pathologists and were known as Body No. 1 and Body No. 2.

Body No. 1, thought to be that of twenty-year-old Mary Rogerson, was incomplete. The neck and trunk were never found, so the exact cause of death couldn't be established. But the tongue was very swollen, which indicated asphyxia.

Body No. 2, thought to be that of Isabella, was more complete. The congested state of the lungs and brain again suggested asphyxia, while the damaged hyoid bone pointed to manual strangulation.

Both bodies had been drained completely of blood, which suggested to the experts that they had been dismembered soon after death.

The pathologists cleaned the remaining tissue away from the two skulls and photographed them from four angles. These photographs were then superimposed over portraits of the two women and the results were staggering, if not conclusive. The defence objected to the photographs being shown to the jury on the grounds that they were "constructed evidence, therefore liable to error."

From the outset of the trial, Norman Birkett must have known he was fighting an uphill battle, because the forensic evidence was overwhelming.

In his final speech to the jury, he said, "It seems scarcely necessary to have to say to you that if you are satisfied of the fact that in the ravine that day were those two bodies, identified beyond the shadow of a doubt, it does not prove this case. If, for example, the word of the prisoner was true when he said, 'They left my house,' there is an end to the case. Even though their bodies were found in a ravine, dismembered, and even though those were the bodies, this does not prove the case against the prisoner.

"The Crown must prove the fact of murder, and you

may have observed much of this case has been pure conjecture. It is not for the defence to prove innocence. It is for the Crown to prove guilt; and it is the duty of the defence to propound a theory which would be satisfactory to your collective minds.

"It is never incumbent upon the prosecution in a charge of murder to prove motive, but they say, 'We will show you the motive; here it is – jealousy because of infidelity.' I ask you to accept with the greatest reserve evidence spoken to after the event, such as that which has been given in this court. The Doctor is arrested for murder, and how that colours the mind.

"This is clear, and I do not seek to deny, that there were intervals and periods of the greatest possible unhappiness. You will remember the phrase used by Dr Ruxton, a phrase so revealing and so powerful: 'We were the kind of people who could neither live with each other, nor live without each other.'

"Unhappiness was no new thing. The Crown described this as a record of marital unhappiness, grievous quarrels; she had left him and then under the persuasion of her sister she had returned. The Prosecution say that at the heart of this family there was this canker, this jealousy; and that this was why he killed her.

"I suggest to you that this is fantastical. To suggest that this was the motive, in my submission, doesn't strengthen their case in any way. On the contrary, it weakens it. For years that unhappiness had existed; and yet there was nothing revealed to you in the evidence which on this occasion should have prompted him to do that which the Crown lay at his charge."

The trial lasted eleven days, but the jury decided Ruxton's fate in a little over an hour. He was sentenced to death and taken to the condemned cell at Strangeways Prison. His subsequent appeal was dismissed and, despite a petition signed by over six thousand people, he was hanged on May 12, 1936.

Most murders leave some mysteries in their wake. But the police were quite confident that they had the answers to the three main questions in this case:

Why did Ruxton kill Isabella? Because he finally allowed jealousy to push him across the thin borderline into madness.

Why did he kill Mary Rogerson? Because she had witnessed the murder of Isabella.

Why did he dismember the bodies? Because he hoped that, in this way, the various pieces would remain undiscovered on the bottom of the river. And that even if a few pieces were found it would be almost impossible to identify them.

The two features of his victims which seemingly worried him most of all were:

1. Mary's squint. . . so he removed the eyes from the skull.

2. Isabella's thunder-thighs. . . so he carved the flesh from the bone.

# 20

# THE BRIDEGROOM

*"What sort of man would want to
kill a nice girl like that?" David Blake in
conversation with a stranger.*

It was Wednesday, October 17, 1934, and autumn had
come early that year. The leaves had fallen from the trees
and the birds had flown to faraway places. And in the
bare and silent woods, a girl lay dead, face down in the
bracken with her pink scarf wrapped tightly around her
neck.

Although this is the season of death, the scene affected
the small group of policemen gathered around her more
deeply than most murders they'd encountered. Even in
death, there was a gentleness and innocence in her face
that touched these men who had become hardened by the
ways of a wicked world.

Police Constable Ebury echoed the thoughts of them
all when he said, "She was too young to die."

A grizzled sergeant nodded. "Aye, she was at that. But
then you're always too young to die this way. Even if
you've only six months left to live, no one has the right to
steal those six months away from you. That's what
murder is really, the worse kind of stealing."

The girl was identified as Emily Yeomans, a 23-year-
old waitress who worked in the County Arcade Cafe in

Leeds. Truth to tell, she hadn't been much of a waitress. She was too much of a dreamer for that. She'd forget some orders and mix up others. But no one had ever minded, for there was sunshine in her smile.

Complete strangers would walk into the cafe, take one look at that smile and feel as though they'd come home. To Emily, the world was a kind and friendly place. . . and it was this trusting nature that had caused her to die so young.

After the medical examiner and the police photographer had completed their chores, her body was taken by ambulance to the morgue. And during that journey, the ambulance passed a church where a wedding was taking place. The extreme contrast. . . sadness and joy. Yet oddly enough there was little evidence of joy on the face of this particular bridegroom, David Blake, a 24-year-old unemployed steel erector.

He had the paleness of a young man who finds the whole experience an ordeal. He nearly dropped the ring and had to be reminded to kiss the blushing bride. Later, Blake slipped away from the wedding reception and bought a copy of the *Yorkshire Evening Post*. He showed the headline on page 12 to his best man, Albert Schofield.

"Leeds cafe waitress found strangled," read Blake. "You remember that girl I said I knew? It's her!"

The honeymoon followed the pattern of the wedding, brief and joyless. Certainly any signs of marital bliss would have been hard to find. In fact on his second night as a married man, Blake sought out the company of a complete stranger named John Jubb and asked whether he could sleep at his house, as he had nowhere else to go.

Jubb, a kindly fellow, agreed albeit with some misgivings; for he was finding Blake's conversation a little morbid. He was seemingly obsessed with the murder of Emily Yeomans.

"What sort of man," he asked, "would want to kill a nice girl like that?"

Jubb asked him how he knew she was a nice girl. Had he perhaps known her?

"Of course not," replied Blake hastily, "that's just what it said about her in the paper."

During the night that followed, Jubb could hear Blake pacing the floor and when the morning came, he had the look of a man who had barely slept at all.

As a gesture of thanks for the night's accommodation, Blake took a box of face powder from his pocket and offered it to him. "Maybe your wife would like this when she returns," he said.

Jubb told him that his wife didn't use powder; but Blake left it on the mantlepiece just the same. Later three waitresses who worked at the County Arcade Cafe would identify that box as the one that had previously belonged to Emily Yeomans. They recognised it, because of the damaged lid.

Blake's obsession with Emily's murder continued. It had become almost his sole topic of conversation; and Jubb wasn't the only one who had begun to have his suspicions. The police were alerted and, just eight days after her death, Blake was arrested.

Hairs from the dead woman's cat were found on his clothes and the box of face powder provided the other key bit of evidence against him.

The trial took place on December 12 before Mr. Justice Goddard. The prosecution was led by Mr. Willoughby Jardine; and the defence by Mr. Paley Scott.

In his opening speech, Mr. Jardine told the jury that Emily Yeomans had been murdered between eight and nine o'clock on the evening of Tuesday, October 16, and that there had been an attempted rape. She had been seen with a man just before that period of time; and Mr. Jardine said he would prove beyond all reasonable doubt that this man was the prisoner, David Blake.

Emily had lived with her uncle, who told the court that he'd seen his niece leave the house and meet a man. But it was dark and so he hadn't seen him clearly.

Emily and the man had also been seen by three boys, but again they were unable to identify him positively.

Next into the witness box came Blake's best man Albert Schofield. The two men had been out drinking on that fateful Tuesday afternoon, a miniature stag night, and Blake had told his best man about a girl named Emily Yeomans. He even admitted he was meeting her later – the evening before his wedding day. When the two revellers parted company at 7.40 p.m., Schofield had seen Blake meet a girl. This time the identification was positive. Schofield was quite sure that the girl was Emily Yeomans.

John Jubb told the jury about his meeting with a stranger who "seemed nervous and talked non-stop about the murder."

By then Blake's cause was hopeless, although Mr. Paley Scott was congratulated by the judge on "one of the most brilliant and courageous defences I've ever heard."

The jury took an hour and a quarter to reach a verdict of guilty and Blake was hanged during the following February.

He had the rare and unenviable distinction of having become a murderer and a bridegroom within the space of twenty-four hours.

# 21

# NO HIDING PLACE

*"She was an affectionate wife, and I was very fond of her." George Smith, speaking of his wife Martha.*

There is no dignity in death. They don't dress corpses. In life, Martha Smith had been the most modest of women. She had been known to blush when the wind lifted her skirt to expose the merest glimpse of thigh. And her dresses were always buttoned all the way to the neck. Other hussies might tantalise their beaux with a display of cleavage. But not Martha. Of that you can be sure.

And yet now this most circumspect of ladies was stretched out naked on a marble slab in the morgue surrounded by a band of men who were viewing her body with the greatest interest. They were police recruits and many of these young innocents were doubtless seeing a nude woman for the very first time. Bear in mind that this was 1905 and that, in those days, the mysteries of the female form remained a secret very much longer than they do today. So a few may have allowed their gaze to linger rather guiltily over the curve of breast and thigh. But the interest of the majority was clinical enough. For even amongst the victims of mayhem, Martha Smith could be deemed as an exceptional case.

She had been stabbed no less than forty times; and the

police inspector in charge of this band of embryo cops had been anxious to show them this example of the kind of frenzy with which a man may sometimes kill.

There had never really been any doubt about the identity of this frenzied killer. As soon as the murder was reported, the police had put out a call for her husband George Smith, and every force in West Yorkshire was on alert for the wanted man.

Two days later, a constable was on duty in Wakefield at five o'clock in the morning when he spotted a man who fitted Smith's description. The man said, "Good morning," cheerfully enough and this enabled the constable to get a closer look. Now he was quite sure. He summoned the assistance of another officer and then stepped in front of the man, saying, "You know what we want you for."

The man, who was indeed George Smith, replied calmly, "Yes, you have got a good cop."

He was taken to Otley, where his clothing was removed and examined. It was found to be covered in dried blood. He had been wearing an handkerchief around his neck and this was later identified as one taken from the scene of the crime.

By now news of his arrest had spread around the town and a large and angry crowd was gathering outside the courthouse. Smith was eventually smuggled out of the back door, because it was feared that he might otherwise have been torn limb from limb.

Another large and hostile crowd arrived on the first day of the trial at the Leeds Assizes. Mr. Justice Jelf warned them on several occasions for booing and hissing the prisoner, but surprisingly didn't clear the court.

Mr. Harold Thomas opened the case for the Crown and told the jury that on the day of the murder, Smith was out of work and being maintained by his wife. Martha had gone into domestic service so that she would be able to provide for her husband and two children.

In June, 1905, she had been working for a Mr. Skelton

in Leeds. Her husband arrived one day and caused a terrible scene, demanding that she should leave. Some days later she did leave, and took her children to her mother's home in Wakefield. She next moved to Ilkley as servant to Mr. and Mrs. Glendenning, who had been away on the day of the murder.

Mr. Skelton, giving evidence, said that one day he found Martha hiding in the pantry. Her face was bruised and she told him that her husband had beaten her up. That same night, Mr. Skelton saw the prisoner and remonstrated with him. Smith promised not to visit the house again, but returned the following day and ordered his wife to leave. She refused and at this, Smith threatened, "I'll swing for you, you bugger." She was, said Mr. Skelton, too terrified to defy him any further.

At this time, Smith had been living in lodgings in Leeds. His landlady, Mrs. Story, told the court that it was Martha who had been paying the rent.

"She came to the house on several occasions," said Mrs. Story, "and appeared both affectionate and generous. She always gave him as much money as she could, perhaps rather more than she could afford."

Later when questioned about Smith's movements on the day of the murder, she said, "Mr. Smith left the house at about a quarter to ten. He told me he was going to Halifax on a job. He was looking quite smart, his clothes were clean and tidy. But after he'd gone, I noticed that a pork-butcher's knife was missing, and I haven't seen that knife since."

Another witness, Miss Beatrice Cryer, told the court that she had been busy gardening on the day of the murder. "At about half-past two," she said, "a man asked me to direct him to the house owned by Mr. Glendenning. I offered him a cup of tea, but he declined saying he was in a hurry."

Asked for a description, she said he was middle-aged and middle-sized. Could she point him out for the benefit of the court? Without a moment's hesitation, she pointed at George Smith in the dock. "That's the man," she said. Had she any doubts? "None at all," she replied firmly and, at this, there was a ripple of applause from the public gallery.

The judge rebuked them, but this appeared to be very much a token gesture. And at this point in the trial, one had the impression that the mood of the public and that of the judge were in tune. . . sympathy for the victim, hatred for the bullying husband.

Margaret Watson, a neighbour of the Glendennings, said that she had seen Martha hanging out washing that afternoon at about four o'clock. Earlier, soon after half-past two, she had spotted a man entering the Glendenning house by the front door.

Miss Glendenning, the daughter of the owners, told the court that she returned home at about half-past six that day and discovered that the back door had been bolted from the inside. She called out, "Martha, let me in," but there was no reply. So she entered the house via the cellar kitchen door and immediately stumbled over Martha's body.

A doctor said he'd found no less than forty wounds on the body which had been inflicted by some sharp instrument. He said that there were pools of blood on the floor, and some on a shelf about four feet away and three and half feet above the ground. The cause of death was haemorrhage from a large wound on the left side of the neck.

This wound was a large gaping one, running from below the angle of the jaw and parallel with it, three inches in length and two and a half inches deep. It divided all the structures of the side of the neck, including the external and internal jugular veins, the external carotid artery, and it had half divided the larynx. Such a wound would have required a considerable amount of force and clearly couldn't have been self-inflicted.

The doctor had arrived at the Glendenning house at half-past seven and estimated that Martha had been dead for two to three hours. As she had been seen alive at four-thirty, this meant that she must have been murdered at some time within the next hour.

George Smith gave evidence and said, "I'm a bricklayer, and about forty-eight years old. I was married to Martha about eleven years ago, and have two children. She was an affectionate wife and I was very fond of her. On the afternoon of September 12, I went to Mr. Glendenning's house and went into the kitchen. I found my missus there and we spoke. She tried to keep me from her, saying she had somebody else. She shoved me away and, as I had a penknife in my hand, I went for her. She went for me and hit me on the shoulder. We had a struggle and I dabbed the knife at her. I don't think she had a knife. She cut my hand as she was taking the knife from me."

Defence counsel Mr. Chapman asked, "Did you do what you did in the heat of the moment?"

Smith: "Yes, I'm very short-tempered."

The judge intervened to ask, "Have you the knife you used against your wife?"

Smith: "No, I threw it away in Ilkley, on the way to the station where I went at about a quarter to six."

Mr. Thomas: "How did your clothes become stained with blood?"

Smith: "I stayed with her until the finish. I kissed her as she lay on the floor, and she kissed me. I got on my knees and I lifted her out of the blood, and put her where she was found. She was not quite dead then."

This remark caused uproar in the court.

Mr. Thomas: "Do you remember cutting her neck across?"

Smith: "I did not do that. I'm sure about it."

Questioned closely by the judge on this point, Smith replied, "I certainly did it, sir. I am simply saying I didn't make such a gash. It was only about one and a half inches long." (more uproar)

Mr. Thomas: "Well, we won't dispute about an inch or

two. Before that, had you given her over forty other wounds?"

Smith: (coolly): "I kept jabbing at her." (hisses)

Judge: "Had she any means of defending herself?"

Smith: "Certainly."

Judge: "What?"

Smith: "Her hands."

Judge: "Is that all, no knife?"

Smith: "I don't think she had. She started the bother with me first." (hisses)

Mr. Thomas: "Was she on the ground when you inflicted this terrible blow?"

Smith: "No, I think she was stood up. About once when she was on the ground I struck her."

Mr. Chapman asked the jury to look upon the case as one of manslaughter. Smith, he claimed, had set out that day with no plan or design to kill his wife.

The jury thought otherwise and took just thirteen minutes to find George Smith guilty of wilful murder.

The judge, in passing sentence, said that this was one of the most brutal murders it had ever been his lot to try, or even hear of. If anything could be added to the wickedness of the whole affair, it was Smith's suggestion that the unfortunate woman had been unfaithful. As far as the evidence went, he could see no grounds for any such accusation. She had been a good, kind wife; and it was very sad indeed to think that Smith had acted so cruelly towards her.

Smith, who received the sentence of death without any show of emotion, was led to the cells amidst a chorus of boos and hisses from the spectators in the public gallery. He was taken to Leeds Prison, where he was hanged twenty-one days later on December 28, 1905. The executioner was Henry Pierrepoint assisted by John Ellis.

# 22

# SENTIMENTAL TOMMY

*"The sooner they hang me the better,
then I shall follow her and be with her."
Fred Ballington's reply to the clerk of the court
when asked how he wished to plead.*

The passengers in the train were having the time of their lives. They were watching a real-life human drama unfold; and as everyone knows, these are vastly more entertaining than their stage counterparts.

There were just two players in the cast. . . Ann Ballington, a pleasantly attractive woman in her late thirties, and her husband Fred, a slightly-built man with a downtrodden look about him.

Ann had stepped into the compartment as soon as the train had stopped at Manchester's London Road station. She had been closely followed by the downtrodden Fred. It was the summer of 1908 and so there was no danger of the drama being cut short by any sudden departure of the train. This was the leisurely age of steam; and engines were wont to take their time in major stations, puffing and snorting, building up the pressure for the journey ahead.

"Couldn't we go to an empty carriage," suggested Fred, "so we can talk privately? Surely you owe me that."

But she would have none of this. "I owe you nothing," she said, "and we've done all the talking we're going to do.

So now please go away and leave me in peace."

Fred shook his head sadly. "All right I'll go away, if that's what you want me to do. But just give me a few shillings, so I can go to Blackpool and find myself a job."

She shook her head firmly. "I've given you too much in the past and it's all gone down the drain. Now I'm giving you nowt."

Fred, who knew how to play up to an audience, appeared to physically reel under this verbal onslaught. And now there was no doubt about it. He had the sympathy vote in that carriage at least.

An elderly gent reached into his pocket, suggesting, "Maybe I can help."

But Ann shook her head more in sorrow than in anger and said, "Anything you give him will be spent in the nearest public house before the night is out. He has forgotten how to work and how to tell the truth. It was a kind thought. But don't worry, I'll help him this one last time."

So saying, she reached into her black bag and gave some coins to her husband. He counted them slowly and then exclaimed, "Eighteen pence! That's no good to me."

He looked around at the other passengers, then gathering his fragile dignity up like a cloak, he said quietly, "All right, I'll say goodbye, and goodbye for ever. Just give me one last kiss to remember you by."

It was perfect melodrama and there wasn't a dry eye in the house. Then he went and spoilt it all. He stepped forward and killed her, stabbing her in the throat. The horrified passengers were rooted to their seats as he turned the clasp knife upon himself and cut his own throat.

Nothing could be done for the unfortunate Ann Ballington and she died where she lay, on the floor of the carriage. But Fred was given first aid and then rushed under police escort to hospital where he later recovered. The police charged him with murder and attempted suicide and he was subsequently tried in July, 1908 before Mr. Justice Bucknill.

## A Date with the Hangman

The melodrama was back in town; for no judge could have been better cast for such a role in a tragic case such as this. He was known affectionately by members of the Bar as 'Sentimental Tommy'. He was a kind and gentle fellow, far too soft-hearted to have become a judge. He spent his days sorrowing for victims and culprits alike. And there was a widespread belief that he was always secretly hoping that his juries would return 'not guilty' verdicts.

On this occasion, the torment for this most unusual judge began with the indictment. When the clerk of the court put the charge of murder to the court, Fred Ballington shocked everyone by shouting out, "Murder! Is she dead then?"

After a long pause, he said quietly, "The sooner they hang me the better, then I shall follow her and be with her."

Clearly he hadn't been told, or hadn't understood, that his wife had died in the train that day; and there could scarcely have been a harsher way of learning such tidings. The judge was visibly upset.

Mr. Spencer Hogg led for the Crown, while Mr. Jordan appeared for Fred Ballington.

Mr. Hogg told the jury that the facts of the tragedy were simple, and that the motive also appeared small and inadequate. "It seemed," he said, "to have been caused by a feeling of annoyance at his wife separating herself from him, and culminating in a feeling of revenge when she would not lend him a sum of money."

He called witnesses to outline the background to the case, explaining that the troubles had really begun when Fred had lost his job. He had started to drink heavily, something he had never been known to do before. As the months went by, the ale began to take a stronger and stronger hold until he would go missing for days at a time. Eventually in May, 1908, Ann Ballington could stand no more. She turned him out of the house and he departed meekly enough and took lodgings nearby. His landlady testified that he had appeared to be a "perfectly quiet and rational man."

Later the same month, he returned to see his wife and asked whether he could stay the night. He had been drinking and so she refused. He then stormed off down the street, shouting and swearing at her.

Then came the fateful afternoon of May 25 at Manchester's London Road station. Witnesses told of the argument which had preceded their entry into the carriage. He was said to have been alternately threatening and pleading with Ann. The argument seemingly centred around his request for money, but no one was quite sure about this.

As Mr. Hogg built up an overwhelming case against him, Fred sat in the dock with head bowed, a broken man with little or no desire to fight for his life. The judge repeatedly looked at him and appeared to grow sadder with each look.

Mr. Jordan didn't call any witnesses for the defence and, in his address to the jury, he said it was open to them to say that the crime was one of manslaughter.

"It would be an insult to your common sense," he said, "to suggest that the prisoner isn't guilty of any crime at all. But on the question of premeditation, I put it to you that my client met his wife that day with no malicious intent."

The jury thought otherwise and found Fred Ballington guilty of wilful murder, after deliberating for just fifteen minutes.

The black cap was placed on the judge's wig and he pronounced the death sentence with tears pouring down his cheeks. As the last words of the sentence were completed, Sir Thomas Bucknill snatched the black cap from his head and hurried from the court, as though the strain had been too much for him to bear.

Fred was led to the cells below, mouthing the word "Goodbye" to the gallery as he went.

He was executed on the morning of July 28, 1908, by

Henry Pierrepoint assisted by William Willis. It was reported that he'd spent a restful last night and eaten a hearty breakfast. At eight o'clock, he'd submitted quietly to the pinioning process and then walked firmly to the scaffold where he died before the clock had finished chiming the hour.

The two hangmen were convinced that this was a man who genuinely welcomed death. So this goes down as one of those very rare cases in which the sentence saddened the judge more profoundly than the prisoner.

# 23

# JEZEBEL

*"You can do what you like, because
when I get out of here I will laugh at you."*
Annie Mayne's remark to Ben Benson.

Charles Mayne was halfway down the corridor when he heard his wife Annie scream. Instinctively he began to run, bursting through her door. Too late, he remembered that he'd heard that particular scream before. It was just that too many months had gone by.

Annie was lying naked on the bed with her legs wrapped around their boss Ben Benson and there was a look of almost unbearable ecstasy in her eyes. The ecstasy was so overwhelming that seconds went by before she became fully aware that her husband was standing there. Benson had turned his head too and his face reflected a mix of shock and uncertainty. After all you can hardly order your odd-job man to leave the room with any authority when you've just been caught in the act of making love to his wife.

But Charles wasn't looking at Benson. He was looking at Annie. He was seeing pure triumph in her eyes. "See," she cried, "I've found myself a real man at last."

Charles was fighting so hard to control the violence within him that his whole body was shaking. He let the silence drag out and then turned to Benson, his voice surprisingly quiet, almost weary. "You've lost yourself a

147

servant," he said, "and gained yourself a woman. . . and you're welcome to her. So don't look upon her as a prize. She'll break your heart the same way she's broken mine. She's an expert at that sort of thing."

And with that, he walked out of the house and out of their lives. Benson had hired the Maynes at the start of the First World War. . . Annie as his housekeeper, Charles as his odd-job man; and both lived in his mansion at Hunslet. Everything had moved smoothly at first; but then Benson had begun to cast amorous eyes over Annie, an attractive man-eater who admitted that no one man could ever totally satisfy her needs. Benson may have made the first move, but you can be sure that she met him more than halfway and they had been lovers long before Charles burst into the bedroom that day.

After his departure, they continued to live together as man and wife. Benson, a strong man, was a lusty lover and seemingly capable of satisfying the demanding needs of Annie. But then in 1916, he packed his bags and decided to go to war. In no time at all, he had been posted to France.

Annie had no intention of sleeping alone and, for her, this would never be a problem. There were a seemingly endless band of volunteers only too anxious to share her bed. So while Benson sploshed through the mud of Flanders, Annie enjoyed life to the full. For a while she led a charmed life.

Whenever Benson came home on leave, her lovers would stay away, enabling her to play the role of dutiful wife welcoming the hero home. And after a fortnight of this, he would return to his unit, weary but otherwise contented.

However on August 26, 1918, Annie's luck finally ran out. Benson arrived home unannounced to find the house empty. Several hours later, Annie returned with a young soldier. They were both drunk and without more ado they headed for the master bedroom. Benson waited downstairs for a while and then quietly began to climb the stairs.

He was halfway up when he heard the same scream that Charles had heard on another day. And pushing open the door, the same sight met his eyes. He chased the half-naked soldier down the road and then came back to confront Annie.

"You're a Jezebel," he shouted. "That's what you are, a Jezebel."

She shrugged. "Well, why shouldn't I be?" she asked. "Men are my pleasure and in this war, a girl needs her pleasures."

The argument ended with Annie sleeping in the master bedroom and Benson on the couch in the living-room. The row was refuelled in the morning when Annie received two letters. Suspecting that they were love letters, he demanded to see them.

Annie refused to hand them over, so he chased her around the kitchen table and hit her with his fist. "I'll do you in," he threatened.

She staggered back, wiped the blood from her lips with the back of her hand and surprisingly smiled. "You can do what you like," she said, "because when I get out of here I will laugh at you. I've had a good time while you've been away and spent the best part of the money your father left you."

In a blind rage, Benson grabbed a razor that was lying by the side of the kitchen sink and cut her throat. She died in hospital the same day.

Benson was tried in December and his defence counsel made great play of the fact that this was a soldier who had come home from the war only to find that he had been betrayed by the woman he loved. The provocation, said counsel Charles Mellor, had been more than flesh and blood could stand. Annie had taunted him until he finally lost all sense of reason.

But this appeal to patriotism failed to save Benson. The jury found him guilty and Mr. Justice Avory sentenced him to death. He was hanged on January 7, 1919. Thomas Pierrepoint was the executioner, assisted by Robert Baxter.

Benson was the first of three soldiers to die on the Armley scaffold on two consecutive days. George Cardwell and Percy Barrett were hanged together the following morning for the 'Pontefract murder'.

# 24

# THE BLACK WIDOW

*"Have you ever heard of a wife poisoning her husband? Look further into the death of Mr. Major of Kirkby-on-Bain." Part of an anonymous letter delivered to the coroner and signed 'Fairplay'.*

She wore her widow's weeds, black from head to foot, and she looked magnificent, head held high, no tears shed, proud and composed despite the loss she had suffered.

Upstairs her husband lay in his open coffin and the mourners tiptoed around her, as they waited for the cortege to arrive at the house. For this was the funeral day. . . Saturday, May 26, 1934, to be precise. . . an odd day for a funeral. But then this had been the widow's choice. "Arthur would have wanted us to put the sad days behind us," she had said. "He would have wanted us to get the burial over quickly, so that we can start living again."

The door bell rang and the widow, expecting the undertakers, opened the door to find two policemen standing there instead. They removed their caps in deference to the occasion.

"We're sorry to intrude on such a day," said the older one, "but we need to talk to you. So if we could just come in for a moment. . ."

A Date with the Hangman

Without a word, she held the door open and they stepped into the hall, both looking immensely embarrassed. The older one, clearly the spokesman, asked, "Could we perhaps see your husband for a moment?"

"My husband is upstairs in his coffin," said the widow.

At this, there was some shuffling of regulation boots, but the older one persisted, "I am sorry about this, madam, truly sorry; but if you could just let us take a quick look, then we'll be gone."

Nothing it seemed could break her composure. She shrugged as though surprised by the vagaries of the human race and simply said, "All right, follow me."

She led them up the stairs and it was as the older policeman looked down at the face of her dead husband that he delivered the bombshell. "I'm afraid," he said, "the funeral will have to be postponed."

"But it's arranged for three o'clock this afternoon," she protested.

"I can't help that. Those are the orders I've been given by my superiors."

There was a long pause and then she asked as calmly as ever, "Do they suspect me of something?"

"Not that I know of," he replied. "But I understand that your husband died rather suddenly."

She broke the news to the waiting mourners and added, "It looks very black against me, as if they were suspicioning me."

Her father nodded soberly. "It looks very much like it," he said.

So began a drama that astonished the farming community of Lincolnshire; for it would have been hard to imagine a less likely suspect in a murder case than Ethel Lillie Major. Her maiden name was Ethel Brown and she had been raised in a family that could have been a counterpart for the Waltons of television fame. . . a happy, caring family that went out of their way to help their neighbours in the quiet country village of Monkton Bottom where her father was the gamekeeper. She had three older brothers whom she cooked and cared for. They in turn treated her fondly as their kid sister and set out to protect her from harm.

But there are some events from which even three strapping brothers can't protect you from. And at the outbreak of the First World War, Ethel became pregnant. She was twenty-three. It was an era in which it was considered a terrible disgrace to be an unmarried mum. But the Brown family had no intention of casting their daughter out into the snow. They rallied around her. Ideally they would have liked her to marry the father of her unborn child. But she steadfastly refused to reveal his identity, and this was a secret she would take with her to the grave. So her parents decided to pretend that the child was theirs and they eventually raised the little girl, Auriel Iris Tryphene, as Ethel's sister.

In January, 1918, Ethel was walking down the village high street when she literally bumped into a soldier. He turned to apologise and he smiled instead. "Good God, it's Ethel," he said.

He was Arthur Major, one of her old school friends, and they hadn't seen each other for five years. He was now serving with the Manchester Regiment and had been wounded on several occasions in France. They celebrated their chance meeting by having lunch together and, in the summer, they were married. They lived with Ethel's parents and Arthur worked as a gardener.

In May, 1920, a son was born and they named him Lawrence. But this event which should have bound them closer together was to have the opposite effect. Arthur appeared to resent his son and refused to show any affection.

In 1929, the Majors rented a bungalow on the outskirts of Horncastle in Lincolnshire. And it was there that a neighbour told Arthur of the true identity of Auriel. When questioned about her so-called 'sister', Ethel admitted the truth. But once again she steadfastly refused to name the father.

Hurt, and feeling very bitter, Arthur turned to drink and the company of other women. He became a drunken bully.

He would beat up his wife from time to time and showed such violence towards his son that Ethel eventually moved the boy into her parents' house to keep him out of harm's way.

Loyalty was the key to her character. She was loyal to the mysterious father of Auriel; and she was loyal after her fashion to Arthur, protecting him from the wrath of her three brothers.

Then on May 24, 1934, Arthur Major died in agony after a short illness. Ethel told the doctor that her husband had died during the night after "having another of his fits." The doctor handed over a death certificate giving the cause of death as 'status epilepticus'. . . a medical term for epilepsy.

In the normal course of events, Arthur would have had a normal burial and that would have been the end of the matter. But in the meantime, the coroner had received an anonymous letter. The author of the letter was never discovered, despite the efforts of the police; but it told a curious story. Signed 'Fairplay', it read:

"Have you ever heard of a wife poisoning her husband? Look further into the death of Mr. Major of Kirkby-on-Bain. Why did he complain of his food tasting nasty and throw it away to a dog, which has since died?

"Ask the undertaker if he looked natural after death. Why did he stiffen so quickly? I myself have heard her threaten to poison him years ago. In the name of the law, I beg you to analyse the contents of his stomach."

This was the letter that halted the funeral at the proverbial eleventh hour and prompted a massive police inquiry. Ethel had told the mourners that "It looks very black against me." And indeed the case against her became blacker day by day.

The dog mentioned in the letter belonged to a next-door neighbour called Mr. Maltby. He had returned home one evening and found his dog obviously in pain. The animal was stiff and couldn't open its mouth. He laid the dog on some sacks, but by the morning it was dead.

Another neighbour, Mrs. Elsie Roberts, told the police that she had seen Ethel feed the dog something off a plate on May 23, the night before Arthur died. According to Mr.

Roberts, Ethel had smiled as the dog ate the scraps, then laughed out loud as she went back into the house. The dog, which Mr. Maltby had buried in his garden, was dug up and handed over to the police for analysis.

Vital organs from both Arthur and the dog were sent to London for analysis. Strychnine was found in the human and animal samples alike. And the police were well aware of the fact that Ethel's father, Tom Brown, had used strychnine to kill vermin during his days as a gamekeeper.

When asked about this, Ethel replied, "I didn't know where he kept his poisons. I never at any time had any poisons in the house."

She then added, "I didn't know my husband died of strychnine." A fatal slip of the tongue; for up until that moment only the police knew which poison had caused Arthur's death.

Tom Brown showed the police a locked box which he kept in his bedroom. Inside there were bottles of strychnine crystals. He said that although his daughter knew the contents of the box, she would have been unable to use them as the key had been missing for years.

A key was eventually found, bright and shiny new, in Ethel's handbag.

On July 8, six weeks after her husband's death, Ethel was charged with his murder. The trial began on October 28 before Mr. Justice Charles. Mr. Richard O'Sullivan led for the Crown, while Mr. Norman Birkett represented the prisoner.

Both the prosecution and the defence used the fact of the unhappy marriage in their cases. The prosecution as a motive, the defence as an excuse. The Crown had three pieces of evidence to rely upon – the key, the dog, and Ethel's slip of the tongue.

Norman Birkett, a masterly advocate, set out to gain the sympathy of the jury. He made great play of the cruel way in which Arthur had treated his family. He spoke eloquently of the loyalty Ethel had given to "this violent bully and womaniser", protecting him from reprisals and attempting to minimise his faults.

Ethel had worn black throughout the trial, as though still mourning her lost husband; and the jury of nine men and three women waited with interest to hear what she had to say, but they were to be disappointed. For some reason best known to herself, she refused to give evidence.

The judge completed his summing up and the jury solemnly filed out of court at twenty-past one. A little over an hour later, they were back. Ethel Major was guilty, with a recommendation for mercy.

It was probably the best that Birkett could have hoped for. Even in the thirties, there was a great reluctance to hang women. . . particularly when a jury had added its plea for mercy.

However he first lodged an appeal on the grounds that the trial judge had summed up unfairly. At the Court of Appeal, the Lord Chief Justice Lord Hewart ruled, "The summing up was perfectly fair and sufficient. The appeal is dismissed."

Mercy was in short supply at the Home Office too. The Home Secretary, Sir John Gilmour, ignored the jury's recommendation and wrote across the case papers that "the law must take its course."

Ethel Lillie Major was duly hanged at Hull Prison on December 19, 1934. Her ghost is said to haunt the prison to this day.

The case leaves several unanswered questions in its wake.

Why in such an apparently open-and-shut case did the police wait six weeks before charging Ethel? Is it possible that they had another suspect in mind?

Who sent the anonymous letter to the coroner? Was it one of those two immediate neighbours, one of Arthur's women – or could it just possibly have been the same mischief-maker who had chosen to reveal Auriel's true relationship to Ethel?

Who was the lover whose name Ethel protected all the way to the grave? And again is it just possible that he provided the real motive behind the murder. . . that she was hoping to exchange a bullying husband for the one genuine love of her life?

# 25

# THE GIGOLO

*"When the mood was upon him, he could
charm the birds out of the trees."
Ellen Maria Westcott talking about her
paramour William Wardell.*

The human race earns its bread in a myriad of different
ways. Millions ride the big trains into the cities, work the
nine-to-five shifts and are given their freedom on Friday
nights. Many obey the dictates of the factory sirens,
trooping in and out of those grim fortresses like rabble
armies. Some toil in the fields. Others slave over hot
stoves and hot typewriters.

But William Wardell had a method of survival
peculiarly his own. Not for him the sweat of the brow, the
need to please the boss or placate the customers. William
Wardell lived off the generosity of the women in his life.
Not to put too fine a point upon it, William Wardell was a
gigolo; and like all gigolos, he was an actor. When it
suited his purpose, he could conjure up a brand of
romance that would touch the hearts of the most sensible
women. Young girls were overwhelmed by his
experienced ways. Mature matrons were treated like
princesses.

He was also an imaginative lover quite capable of
making all their previous sexual adventures appear

mundane and second-rate by comparison. In return for these favours, he expected his women to keep him in the style to which he had become accustomed; and most of them did. Indeed in his entire life there is no record of him ever having been gainfully employed. . . that is, unless you consider 'gigolo' to be an occupation.

His major paramour was Ellen Maria Westcott, a neat, hard-working and trusting lady who in 1908 opened a boarding house in Bradford for theatrical artists. She was fond of saying that "When the mood was upon him, Bill could charm the birds out of the trees." He was wont to use that charm upon some of the more decorative ladies from the local theatre who boarded under Maria's roof. . . a habit that tested her patience to the limit. Finally after thirteen years and countless affairs, her patience ran out, and so did she!

But for Wardell, the line of gullible ladies was seemingly endless; and in no time at all, he had persuaded Hilda Kidd, another pleasant and trusting woman, to care for his various needs. However the twenties were an age of depression and with the best will in the world, Hilda couldn't satisfy all of his expensive tastes. So he began looking around for another pigeon to pluck; and it was then that Elizabeth Reaney, a sixty-year-old widow, loomed up as the answer to his prayers.

She owned her own house, had money in the bank and she was lonely. . . the essential qualifications for a pigeon. Wardell introduced himself as George Goodson, an engineer who lived in Leeds. He'd had a succession of aliases. He proceeded to court Elizabeth Reaney in the old-fashioned way, bunches of flowers, car rides to the country tea houses and all the trimmings. To her, he was the real-life hero from some romantic novel. She was totally captivated and when he suggested marriage, she didn't hesitate. They decided to buy a house in Derbyshire and start a new life together.

The task of searching for property in Derbyshire was left to Wardell and in no time at all, he was telling her that he'd found an ideal cottage in Buxton at a price that was just right.

The widow was overjoyed at the news. She looked at the documents he'd brought and announced that she would buy without looking, as she trusted her friend completely. This was, of course, Wardell's forte. Women had always trusted him, to their cost.

She sold her own house and vacant possession was to be given on Saturday, February 23, 1924. During that month, Wardell agreed to move some of the smaller items of furniture to Buxton in his car. The rest would go in a removal van.

The removal men arrived on the Saturday at the appointed hour and found a note pinned to the front door, telling them to return on Monday as Mrs. Reaney had gone to Buxton on urgent business.

They were just about to leave when a car drew up. The new owners had arrived to make sure that everything would be left secure. The widow's sudden change of plan worried them all and after some discussion, they decided to break into the house through the cellar and have a look around.

Almost immediately one of the removal men stumbled over the dead body of Elizabeth Reaney. Her head had been savagely battered. The police made house-to-house enquiries in the area and were given a description of the man with whom the widow had been hoping to start a new life. . . a man known to the neighbours as George Goodson.

This description was circulated in the north of England via newspapers and posters with the announcement that the police wished to interview the man fitting this description.

The landlord of the Peel Inn in Bradford spotted the item in his local paper and remarked to customers that it fitted one of his regulars, William Wardell. It was an odd remark, because this description of a tall, slim, rather distinguished-looking middle-aged man could have fitted at least ten thousand others. One can only suppose that he had already formed his own suspicions of Wardell.

When Wardell next visited the pub, the landlord advised him to go to the police and clear himself. "Otherwise," said the landlord, "there's the danger that someone could steer them in your direction, and it could look black against you."

Wardell shrugged, casual as you please. "Good idea," he said. "I'll finish this drink first and then I'll go and talk to them."

In the same confident mood, he went to the local police station and made a long and detailed statement. He was asked to remain at the station, while his story was being checked out. It was soon discovered that the statement was nothing more than a pack of lies. He was again interviewed at length, and eventually charged with murder.

On May 8, 1924, Wardell stood in the dock before the icily severe Mr. Justice Avory, a judge capable of putting fear into the hearts of the most hardened criminals. But Wardell, dressed in a faded blue suit, seemed unimpressed and maintained an air of indifference throughout the trial. Mr. C.F. Lowenthal led for the prosecution and Mr. C.J. Frankland headed the defence team.

Mr. Lowenthal, opening the case, said that this murder of an inoffensive old woman had been carried out with the worst possible motive, the motive of robbery. She was not a woman who could have had any physical attraction for Wardell. His only interest, suggested Mr. Lowenthal, lay in the money she possessed. He had visited her frequently, but taken great care to conceal his true identity. Four letters had been found but all four bore a false name and a false address. The name adopted was 'Goodson', the address 'Leeds'. The postmark on three of the letters was, however, Bradford.

Mr. Lowenthal read the letters to the jury, then called his witnesses. The first of these, Maria Westcott, said she had known Wardell for about thirty years and lived with him until December, 1921. The four letters were placed before her in the witness box and she immediately identified the handwriting as Wardell's.

Hilda Kidd was asked to confirm that she had also lived with the prisoner, William Wardell. She hesitated a long time before answering and the question was repeated. She pointed at Wardell. "That's the man I lived with," she said, "but I knew him as Bill Stamford, nor Wardell."

In answer to another question, she said, "He had an evening job. He used to bring home pieces of furniture after dark. He told me they came from a friend's house." The 'pieces of furniture' were later identified as items which had belonged to Mrs. Reaney. . . items which he had been officially transporting to their non-existent cottage in Buxton.

Dr. Hayes-Smith, a police surgeon, said that Mrs. Reaney had received four heavy blows on the head and that a hammer was the most probable weapon. He thought it unlikely that the murderer would have been splashed with blood. He drew this conclusion from the lack of blood on the hammer shaft that was removed from the dead woman's house.

Bernard Pickles, the landlord of the Peel Inn, told the court that on February 18, he'd changed a five-pound note for the prisoner. He had noticed that, in addition to this note, Wardell had a further twenty pounds in his wallet. . . in that day and age, a considerable sum.

On the second day of the trial, the Crown called Gerald Gurrin, a handwriting expert. He explained in great detail the comparisons he had made between known specimens of the prisoner's handwriting and those from the 'Goodson' letters found in Mrs. Reaney's house. He was satisfied, he said, that they were written by the same person. The note, pinned to the front door for the removal men, was also penned by the same hand.

This was the most damning evidence so far and Mr. Frankland was quick to cross-examine. He asked Mr.

Gurrin, "Speaking only as a handwriting expert, are you prepared to swear definitely that Exhibit 27 (the note on the door) was written by Wardell?"

Mr. Gurrin hesitated. "I am not prepared to swear definitely," he said. "But I find it very difficult to conceive that it could have been written by anyone else. The note contains only a small amount of material, but the number of similarities are striking."

Altogether the Crown called fifty-three witnesses. But when the defence completed their own case, they informed the judge that they wouldn't be calling any witnesses.

Mr. Lowenthal then addressed the jury, pointing out that the facts submitted by him in his opening speech had been borne out by the evidence.

There was one difference, however, the jury had now had the opportunity to compare the handwriting of the accused with that of the 'Goodson' letters and so to judge for themselves who was the true author and who was not. On the evidence before them, Mr. Lowenthal asked the jury to record a verdict of wilful murder.

For the defence, Mr. Frankland said that no one could dispute that the unfortunate woman had been murdered. The only issue was the connection between this horrible crime and the man accused of it.

It had been said that the motive was robbery. If so, then the robber had to be the most amazingly stupid person and the most appalling blunderer. Certainly it would have been hard to believe that it could be the prisoner, for as far as could be ascertained he hadn't taken from that house one single penny or one single article of value.

Mr. Frankland referred to the evidence regarding the handwriting. He asked the jury not to make up their minds as the result of examining photographs, but to consider only the original documents.

"As for the note pinned to the door, I urge you to put it side-by-side with Wardell's letters and on the basis of that comparison, and that only, make up your minds."

Finally he said, "I don't suggest that Wardell is a plaster saint but the fact that a man has done shameful things in the past has nothing to do with the present. The whole case against Wardell is one of suspicion and suspicion only. Therefore there can only be one verdict. . . Not Guilty."

Mr. Justice Avory, summing up, said the case was one of circumstantial evidence as opposed to what is known as direct evidence. It was not less reliable on that account; for, as had often been said, circumstances cannot lie. The jury had to ask themselves whether any other person than the accused could have committed the crime. There was no evidence to suggest that the house had been broken into prior to the body being found. So the crime, it would appear, had been committed by someone who had entered the house with the consent of Mrs. Reaney. . . someone she trusted.

The summing-up occupied an hour and a half, and the jury retired at 12.45 p.m. on Saturday, May 10, 1924, the third day of the trial. After an absence of just over an hour, they returned with a verdict of guilty. Wardell listened to that verdict unmoved, only glancing casually at the foreman as he announced the dreaded word.

His Lordship, addressing the convicted man, said, "William Horsley Wardell I entirely concur with the verdict of the jury. I have no doubt that you deceived this woman into the belief that you were going to marry her and take her to Buxton, then you foully and brutally murdered her, in the hope of possessing yourself of the money she had."

The judge then passed sentence of death, and Wardell was led below to the cells by two prison officers. An actor to the end, he gave a mock bow to an attractive woman leaning over the rail in the public gallery.

His subsequent appeal was dismissed, and he was hanged on June 18, 1924. Thomas Pierrepoint and William Willis were the executioners.

There can be little doubt about his guilt. By leaving the note pinned to the door, he virtually signed his own death warrant. But the motive behind the murder will remain for ever a mystery.

This was an apt parallel of the goose who laid the golden eggs. By killing this unfortunate widow, Wardell had seemingly cast aside the prospect of a life of ease, and gained nothing in return.

Was there perhaps more to the act than meets the eye? Had Elizabeth Reaney perhaps discovered at the eleventh hour that her romantic lover was simply a trickster? Or had the gigolo maybe discovered another pigeon who would have been more to his taste?

# 26

# KILLARNEY KATE

*"Mighty King. Have pity on your lowly, afflicted subject.*
*Don't let them kill me on Wednesday."*
*Charlotte Bryant's plea to King Edward VIII.*

On the eve of her execution in 1936, Charlotte Bryant wrote a last letter with a tantalising message: "It's all......'s fault I'm here. I listened to the tales I was told."

That missing word was blotted out on the orders of the prison governor. And so the real truth behind one of the most intriguing murders of the twentieth century may never be known. Did this good-time girl have an accomplice or is it just possible that she was, as she claimed, the innocent party?

Her story really began in 1922 in Londonderry where, as Charlotte McHugh, she became the darling of the British troops garrisoned in that unhappy country during the Black and Tan troubles. With her raven-black hair and flashing eyes, she was something to capture the imagination of a man. . . particularly if he happened to be a soldier a long way from home. Because of that striking black hair, they called her 'Darkie' and made her the unofficial mascot of the regiment. She loved the attention and was free with her favours. Much too free for the liking of some of the Irish militants.

On one occasion she was surrounded in a bar by some

of the local hotheads who were threatening to tar and feather her. . . the punishment traditionally meted out to Irish girls who dared to fraternise with the enemy. The mob was led by Sean Kelly, one of the early Republican leaders. Incredibly she appeared to enjoy the situation.

"Do you mean, Sean," she asked, "that you'd be willing to strip a poor innocent girl like me?"

"To be sure we would," said Kelly. "Any girl who betrays her kith and kin deserves nothing less." At this, there was a murmur of approval from the mob.

Her eyes opened even wider. "Are you saying that although I'd be begging you not to, you'd then brush on the tar and cover me in feathers?"

"That's what we're saying," said Kelly grimly and by now the murmur of the mob had turned into a growl.

"And would you then," she asked, "tie me to a rail and parade me naked through the streets?"

"That too," replied Kelly, "and maybe tonight should be the night."

But far from being scared by the threats, she openly taunted the mob. "Promises, promises," she said, beginning to laugh, well aware of the fact that there were enough soldiers in the bar to ensure that she couldn't suffer such a fate on this night at least.

The arrival of the troops had brought some much-needed excitement into her life and widened her dreams. Up until then, her life had been drab. She had never learnt to read or write, so the chance of obtaining a decent job was remote. Yet she still hungered for the good times and most of all she hungered for England. After all, weren't the streets of London paved with gold?

So she viewed her soldier lovers with a calculating eye, wondering which of them would be willing to take her with him across the Irish Sea once their tour of duty had been completed. Her choice finally fell on Frederick Bryant, a military policeman in the Dorset Regiment. He was an easy-going country boy who had served in the latter stages of the First World War and been wounded in the leg. He was overwhelmed by this bold beauty and only too delighted to take her back to England.

They were married at Wells in Somerset and, in 1925, he was taken on as a cowman on a farm at Over Compton about two miles from Yeovil. The work was poorly paid, but at least his employer provided a tied cottage for the couple to live in. It was a far cry from the bright lights she had dreamed about. Charlotte bore five children during their marriage, but she wasn't content to remain simply a housewife and mother. Life in the barrack town of Londonderry had given her a taste for men that no one man could hope to satisfy. She started visiting the lunch-time pubs, picking up men and taking them back to the cottage while Fred was working in the fields.

She became known variously as 'Compton Liz', 'Black Bess' and 'Killarney Kate', and the entire surrounding countryside was pleasantly scandalised by her lifestyle. She was at the very least a part-time prostitute. But it seems likely that the sex was more important to her than the money, which of course made her a very unusual prostitute. When a client was expected, she would send her children to the village to buy sweets. As this was some two miles from her home, it gave her ample time to earn her fee. . . and in the eyes of the neighbours, this was yet another strike against her.

There may well have been some envy in all this; for she was able to afford several luxuries beyond the reach of others. Salmon, cream and bottles of spirits, for instance, were regular items on her shopping list. When a neighbour raised the subject of Charlotte's immoral lifestyle, her husband Fred simply shrugged and said, "I don't care what she does. Four pounds a week is better than thirty shillings."

In December 1933, Charlotte met a gypsy who called himself Bill Moss, but whose real name was Leonard Edward Parsons. To her, he cut a romantic figure with his swarthy good looks and flamboyant ways. He had just left his gypsy lover, Priscilla Loveridge, who had borne him four children during the eleven years they had lived together. That Christmas, Charlotte invited Parsons to the cottage and he shared Christmas dinner with her husband and children.

The two men struck up an instant friendship and when Parsons complained about his lodgings, Fred invited him to stay with them at the cottage. It was a generous but foolish invitation, for the cottage with its four rooms was barely large enough to house the Bryants let alone a lodger. Parsons accepted happily enough and spent the night on the sofa in the living-room.

It was a strange relationship, for Fred must have realised that as soon as he left the cottage to begin his day's work, Parsons would slip into bed with Charlotte. As a result of all this, the unfortunate Fred was sacked and turfed out of the cottage. The farmer he worked for said flatly that he had no intention of encouraging such scandalous goings-on.

Fred took a farm-labouring job at Coombe, a village just outside Sherbourne; and astonishingly the previous domestic pattern was repeated. Leonard Parsons joined them and now there was no longer any pretence. Charlotte and her gypsy lover slept in the main bed, and Fred slept on the sofa. Eventually even this mild-mannered husband rebelled and ordered Parsons to leave. . .

"If Leonard goes, I go too," said Charlotte.

Fred nodded soberly. "That's up to you," he said.

Taken aback by this change of manner, she packed a few meagre belongings into a bag and taking two of the children, Lily and Billy, by the hand, she left the cottage and followed her lover out of the house. They rented rooms in Dorchester for two nights, but Charlotte was already regretting the rashness of her actions and soon she was on a bus heading home for Coombe.

She told Fred that she'd been missing the children she had left behind and he forgave her instantly. "My husband was pleased to see me," she said later.

But like the proverbial bad penny, Parsons also

returned and once more the easy-going Fred relented and allowed him to stay. The two men were frequently seen together in the local pub and appeared to be on the best of terms. Then Charlotte became pregnant by her lover. It was around this time that Fred started suffering from his mysterious 'gastric attacks'.

The first came in May, 1935. Charlotte had gone out for the day with Parsons, leaving her husband's lunch in the oven. Almost as soon as he'd finished the meal, Fred cried out in agony and rolled off his chair. A neighbour found him sitting on the stairs, doubled up and ashen-faced. He gave him salt water to make him sick and called a doctor. The doctor diagnosed gastro-enteritis and four days later, Fred returned to work. Three months later, Fred had another attack and once more the doctor called it gastro-enteritis.

Soon afterwards Parsons decided to leave, saying it was hard to ply his trade, mainly horse dealing, in the area. Charlotte was furious and refused to let him take his belongings, but he went just the same.

But if Fred Bryant hoped that this heralded a more peaceful era, he was to be disappointed. For Charlotte had found a new friend, Lucy Mavina Ostler, a widow with seven children. . . and she wanted this new-found friend to move into the house with her seven children. The long-suffering Fred vetoed the idea and this time he seemed determined to stand firm.

But on the night of December 21, Mrs. Ostler did spend the night in the cottage, after Charlotte had complained of feeling nervous. During the night, Fred was suddenly taken ill and the following morning he was rushed to the local hospital. Twelve hours later, he was dead. The autopsy revealed acute arsenic poisoning.

The police arranged for Charlotte and her children to stay at an institution, while they searched the cottage for evidence. The search lasted seven weeks and at the end of that time the police were scarcely any wiser. Their main suspects were the two women who had spent that fateful night in the cottage, but there was still nothing in the way of evidence likely to impress a judge and jury.

Then a pharmacist in nearby Yeovil reported that he had sold a tin of arsenic weedkiller to a woman who had signed the poison register with a cross. Charlotte and Lucy Ostler were asked to take part in an identity parade, but the pharmacist failed to recognise either.

However the parade had frightened Mrs. Ostler and she began to talk. She told the police that shortly after Fred's death, Charlotte had pointed to a green tin in the cupboard and said, "I must get rid of that." Her description of the tin matched that of the one sold by the pharmacist in Yeovil. Mrs. Ostler also said that a few days later while raking the ashes under Charlotte's boiler, she had found a burnt tin of the same size and thrown it into the yard.

The police were delighted, for they had found a bent and charred tin which fitted this description. It had also contained traces of arsenic.

Charlotte was promptly charged with the wilful murder of her husband and on May 27, 1936, appeared before Mr. Justice MacKinnon, a kindly judge who would find this trial a considerable ordeal. The Crown brought in the big guns, headed by the Solicitor General, Sir Terence O'Connor. The defence was put in the capable hands of Mr. J.D. Casswell.

From the beginning, the odds seemed cruelly stacked against the prisoner. At thirty-three, she was no longer the ravishing beauty who had bewitched the troops in Londonderry. She had allowed that raven-black hair to become bedraggled. Her clothes were threadbare and ill-fitting; and her unkempt looks were those of a woman who had lost all pride. As the trial developed, she became increasingly isolated, increasingly betrayed. Lucy Ostler, the friend to whom she had offered shelter, appeared as chief witness for the prosecution. Leonard Parsons, her gypsy lover, added his damning testimony to the rest. And even her children, Lily, aged ten, and Ernest, aged twelve, were led into the witness box to testify against their mother.

Yet the prosecution still had its problems. There was no direct evidence to link Charlotte with her husband's death. True, they had found the tin containing arsenic; but this wasn't an unusual find in a farming community where poisons for pests were fairly commonplace. And the police had also failed to prove that this particular tin had been purchased by Charlotte.

The Crown's case was further weakened by the fact that there had been two women in the cottage that night, each with an equal opportunity of poisoning the unfortunate Fred.

So Sir Terence O'Connor elected to base much of his case on what he described as "the prisoner's strong motive for destroying her husband in order that her marriage might be at an end." There was, he said, "what dramatic writers call the eternal triangle. . . and it was not absent from this case." In other words, he was suggesting that Charlotte had murdered Fred so that she could be free to live happily ever after with Leonard Parsons.

Lucy Ostler came into the witness box, looking unusually tidy and respectable in marked contrast to Charlotte who sat just a few feet away. She explained that she had chosen to stay in the cottage on that fateful night solely to please Charlotte who had "complained of being nervous." They had all retired for the night at the early hour of seven. Fred was already ill and Charlotte and the baby had joined him in the main bed. Mrs. Ostler had bedded down in the armchair which was in the same room. In the small hours, she claimed to have heard Charlotte trying to persuade her husband to take a drink of Oxo. She wasn't sure whether he drank this, as it was dark; but a few minutes later, she heard him vomiting.

She said that Charlotte had cried once she realised that Fred was dead and asked her what an inquest was. She had replied, "I think it's a kind of operation and if you can't read nor write, nothing can be found."

On another occasion, Charlotte had told her that she hated her husband. At this, Mrs. Ostler had said, "In that case, why don't you go away with Parsons, Lottie, and not bear malice to your husband?"

Charlotte had shrugged and said, "I don't want to leave the children. That's why."

Unlike Charlotte who could neither read nor write, Mrs. Ostler could understand the written word and would often read out loud the titbits from newspapers and magazines for the benefit of her friend. One particular item had concerned the trial in America of Frances Creighton ('The Lucretia Borgia of Long Island'). According to Mrs. Ostler, Charlotte had shown great interest in this and asked, "How would I get rid of someone?"

As the evidence built up, Charlotte stared at her former friend in seeming disbelief, clearly shocked by this betrayal. But even worse was to follow as Mrs. Ostler related, "A few days after Fred's death, I saw a tin with green markings on it in the kitchen. The word 'poison' was written on the lid. Charlotte said she would have to get rid of it and took it out into the garden, saying that she intended to burn some rubbish." The police had, of course, found just such a tin and Mrs. Ostler identified this as the same one she had seen in the kitchen.

In his memoirs (*A Lance for Liberty*) Mr. Casswell referred to the tense moment when he rose to cross-examine Mrs. Ostler. "The utmost I could hope to do," he wrote, "was to raise a reasonable doubt in the minds of the jury as to whether Mrs. Ostler and not Mrs. Bryant should have been in the dock."

It seemed fairly clear that one of the two women had poisoned Fred, and Mrs. Ostler reluctantly agreed that she had had an equal opportunity of administering the fatal dose. She also agreed that she had helped to nurse the sick man, even giving him medicine.

Mr. Casswell: "You realise that the evidence you have been giving is very unfavourable to Mrs. Bryant?"

Mrs. Ostler: "I do."

Mr. Casswell: "I suggest that the story of the tin is a falsehood."

Mrs. Ostler: "It is not."

Mr. Casswell: "I suggest that you were rather frightened."

Mrs. Ostler: "I had nothing to be frightened of."

Mr. Casswell: "Did you say on one occasion that Mrs. Bryant *never* told you that she wanted her husband out of the way?"

Mrs. Ostler: "No, I never made any such statement."

But Mr. Casswell pressed on cleverly and managed to get her to admit that she had been frightened by being put on an identification parade in front of the chemist. She had also been nervous about the view the police might take of her presence in the cottage on the fateful night. But she denied that this had been the reason why she had been so willing to implicate Charlotte.

Likewise, she denied that she had wanted to share the cottage with her children, or that Fred had objected to this. Mr. Casswell had been most anxious to plant that particular thought in the minds of the jury, because this would have been her most logical motive for murder. Despite the denials, he had at least planted a few doubts.

But his success was short-lived. The Crown had chosen their witnesses well. An insurance agent who had visited Fred after the first of those mysterious illnesses said that, "He looked like a man who had not much longer to live. His eyes were bulgy and he looked wasted and thin. I would never have insured him."

Mr. Priddle, Fred's employer, had called at the cottage on the day he died. He said, "I looked through the window and I could see him vomiting and retching. Mrs. Bryant told me he had been like that since seven that morning. She was standing there with her arms folded."

There was a sense of outrage when Charlotte's two eldest children, Lily and Ernest, were led into the box. Many of the lawyers and public alike felt that it was unfair to subject them to such an ordeal.

A small blue bottle was passed to Lily and she was asked, "Did you ever see Mr. Parsons with that bottle?"

Lily: "Yes, sir. He poured it out on the stone outside and said to Mummy, 'If you don't look out, I'll ram that down your throat.' "

Sir Terence: "Did you notice anything that happened when it was poured on the stone?"

Lily: "Yes, it fizzled all up."

While the children were giving evidence, Mr. Justice Mackinnon bowed his head, clearly distressed, and Charlotte wept.

But the sight of Leonard Parsons stepping into the witness box seemed to shock her even more; for this she obviously regarded as the greatest betrayal of them all. He looked what he was, a gypsy pedlar, a weatherbeaten man of the great outdoors, coarse-featured and unshaven.

There was a moment of low comedy when Sir Terence, a very upper-crust lawyer, questioned him about his relationship with Charlotte.

Sir Terence: "Had you been intimate with Mrs. Bryant?"

Parsons: "I can't understand."

Sir Terence: "Did you live with her as man and wife?"

Parsons: "No."

As Sir Terence was basing much of his case on the eternal triangle motive, this was scarcely the answer he'd been hoping to hear. But realising the Parsons's grasp of the English language was limited, he adopted a more down-to-earth approach.

Sir Terence: "Did you and Mrs. Bryant have sexual intercourse?"

Parsons: "Oh yes, a lot, from the time we met until the day I left."

Sir Terence breathed a sigh of audible relief and then switched the questioning to an equally damaging subject for the prisoner.

Sir Terence: "Have you ever had any weed-killer?"

Parsons: "No."

Sir Terence: "Or taken any to Mr. and Mrs. Bryant's cottage?"

Parsons: "No."

Sir Terence: "But you do recall an incident concerning weed-killer?"

Parsons: "Yes. One day in August, 1935, I was standing outside the kitchen door when I heard Mr. Bryant say to his wife, 'What's this?' Mrs. Bryant replied, 'That's weed-killer.' "

In cross-examination, Mr. Casswell got Parsons to admit that he hadn't actually seen the tin in question. . . and for that matter, had no means of knowing that it was a tin at all.

He then switched the questioning in a bid to undermine the Crown's claim that Parsons was Charlotte's motive for murdering her husband.

Mr. Casswell: "Are you telling my lord and the jury that you are the sort of man Mrs. Bryant would want to marry, knowing that you had four illegitimate children you couldn't afford to keep, that you had no fixed home and were travelling about the country hawking?"

Parsons: "We were on good terms."

This remark was such a remarkable understatement of the situation that even the judge smiled. More much needed light relief came with the appearance of Parsons' gypsy 'wife' Priscilla Loveridge and her mother, the formidable Mrs. Penfold. Priscilla wore a moleskin coat and a lot of costume jewellery. She used bad language and clearly enjoyed her hour upon the stage. Mr. Justice MacKinnon didn't share in her enjoyment, finding it well-nigh impossible to control her.

She repeated what she had once said to Charlotte: "I hope your husband soon gets better and gives you and Parsons a damn good hiding."

Mrs. Penfold, wearing a man's trilby hat, was equally happy to be in centre stage. She also repeated words she had once spoken to Charlotte: "If I thought you had told me lies, I would break your neck."

The scientific evidence was presented by Dr. Gerald Roche Lynch, the Home Office's senior analyst. Traces of arsenic amounting to 4.09 grains had been found in Bryant's body. There was also arsenic in his hair and fingernails which denoted that he had been fed poison over a long period. Samples of dust taken from the bedroom in the cottage had been found to contain arsenic and the poison had also been present in the burnt-out tin found amongst the garden rubbish and in the boiler ash.

The ashes contained 149 parts per million of arsenic which was, said Dr. Roche Lynch, "abnormally large" and strongly suggested that something containing arsenic had been put in the fire. The usual amount of arsenic found in ash, he told the jury, was about 45 parts per million. It was a statement that would come back to haunt the good doctor.

The Crown had produced over thirty witnesses; and although some had been discredited, the sheer numbers weighed heavily against Charlotte. So somewhat against his better judgment, Mr. Casswell decided to put her in the witness box in the hope that she could refute some of the charges made against her. So her evidence consisted mainly of denying what others had said about her.

When questioned about Lucy Ostler's evidence, she showed her sense of betrayal by saying, "We were very good friends. I have never done her any harm." With that went the unasked question, "So why does she now want to harm me?"

Her account of the events on the fateful night differed from Mrs. Ostler's insomuch as she claimed to have slept though the long night. "I went to bed early," she said, "because I was completely fagged out, and I slept right round until seven the next morning." She added that at breakfast, she was told Mrs. Ostler had gone to Fred's aid several times during the night when he asked for water.

Charlotte denied that she had ever bought any poison or weed-killer. "I can't tell you poison," was as strong a denial as her grasp of language would permit. The very naivety of that statement lent it a certain strength.

When asked about traces of arsenic found in the pockets of one of her coats, she replied simply, "I don't know anything about that, sir."

The suggestion was that she had worn this coat during a visit to town and had carried the weed-killer home in her pocket. The clerk of the court held up the coat. It was blue and had a button missing. Charlotte admitted that it was hers, but explained, "It's too small for me. I would never have worn it into town."

Anxious to demonstrate the point, she took off the brown coat with the fur collar which she was wearing and prepared to put on the blue one. To show that the test was a fair one, she also slipped off the cardigan she had been wearing over her tight-fitting black dress. As a result, the entire courtroom could see clearly that the blue coat was indeed too small for her. She did a little pirouette for the benefit of the jury. . . and for that moment, at least, she had the sympathy of the court.

When questioned by Sir Terence about her relationship with Parsons, she admitted that her original statement to the police wasn't entirely true. "I don't like to tell them everything," she explained. "I was embarrassed."

"A mistake is a mistake," said Sir Terence, but then added severely, "I'm talking about deliberate lies."

Mr. Casswell wasn't impressed with the prosecution's suggestion that her motive for poisoning Fred was simply to get him out of the way so that she would be free to marry Parsons. He pointed out to the jury that Fred was far from being a jealous man. On the contrary, he had almost encouraged Parsons to make love to his wife.

Charlotte had admitted freely that she had gone away with her gypsy lover on several occasions and that they had stayed overnight at such towns as Dorchester, Plymouth and Weymouth. But she had always returned to Fred and there had been no arguments over this. It had been suggested that Parsons had tired of Charlotte, but she would have none of this. . . "I wasn't sorry to see the last of him," she said. "I didn't want the man."

In his summing up, the judge told the jury that there were two questions to be answered: "Did Bryant die of arsenic poisoning?" and "If he did, was the poison administered by his wife?"

He listed the dates of Fred's three mysterious 'gastric attacks' and reminded the jury of those who had been in the cottage on those occasions. In May and August, both Parsons and Charlotte were there; and in December, Mrs. Ostler and Charlotte had spent the night in the same room as the murdered man. The fact that Charlotte had been there on all three occasions weighed heavily against her.

As Mr. Casswell wrote later, "The Crown's evidence had been so weighty that I did not really doubt what the jury's verdict would be."

The jury retired for an hour and when they returned several were showing signs of distress. The foreman was so overcome that he had difficulty in uttering the single word, "Guilty".

Charlotte was surprisingly calm and responded to the verdict by saying quietly, "I am not guilty."

The judge echoed the jury's emotions and almost broke down as he pronounced the death sentence. It was then and only then that the full gravity of the situation appeared to be accepted by the prisoner. Her head sank and she began to sob loudly. She had to be supported in a semi-collapsed condition to the cells below.

Mr. Casswell had also found the case and the verdict depressing. He spent the weekend with his wife and eldest son at Lyme Regis; and admitted in his memoirs that no other trial had ever left him quite so tired, quite so weary, as this one. But upon returning to London on the Monday, he found a letter waiting for him in chambers which immediately raised his hopes. It came from Professor William A. Bone of the Imperial College of Science and Technology and read:

*Dear Sir,*

*If I am right in supposing that you were the Defending Counsel in the case of Rex v Bryant which ended at the Dorchester Assizes on Saturday last, would you please communicate with me as soon as possible because I have something to put before you, arising out of that part of evidence in the learned judge's summing up relating to the normal percentage of arsenic in coal ashes, which I think may possibly have an important bearing upon the ultimate issue. And I would be glad of an opportunity of putting it before you in the interest of justice.*

*Perhaps I should add that I have had nothing at all to do with the case but as a scientific authority on coal I was struck by a statement in the Sunday Times to the effect that in his summing up the learned judge had recalled how Dr. Roche Lynch had stated that coal ashes normally contain 45-50 parts per million arsenic and that the ashes from the copper had 149 parts per million. And I should like to have an opportunity of discussing the matter with you.*

Yours faithfully,
William A. Bone, DSc, FRS

Caswell immediately rang the professor who told him that Dr. Roche Lynch's evidence on the proportion of arsenic normally found in the ashes of domestic fires was wrong. It had been established that the normal content was at least 140 parts per million and usually nearer 1,000 parts per million. Consequently the arsenic found in the boiler ash at the Bryant's cottage was actually well below the level of what would normally have been expected. The effect of this new evidence, as Mr. Casswell wrote later, was "to directly refute the account given my Mrs. Ostler in the witness box."

Professor Bone gave a signed statement confirming everything he had said and Casswell included this in his grounds of appeal. He also took the unusual step of asking the Court of Criminal Appeal to hear the professor's additional evidence in the interests of justice. . .

The hearing took place in London on June 29, 1936. In the corridor outside the courtroom, Sir Terence O'Connor confided to Casswell, "Lynch has certainly made a dreadful blunder. He knew nothing about the contents of coal himself, but got his information over the telephone. He must have misheard what was said. It's quite obvious that he was wrong and you were right."

In his own words, Casswell "walked into court with a lightened step". But his hopes were swiftly dashed. The Lord Chief Justice, Lord Hewart, sitting with Mr. Justice Finlay and Mr. Justice Humphreys, refused to hear Professor Bone who was waiting outside the court.

Lord Hewart told the defence lawyers that the application was "objectionable" and stated, "The Court will not listen to the opinion of scientific gentlemen bringing their minds to bear on evidence which they have not heard." He went on to say, "This Court sets its face like flint against attempts to call evidence which could have been made available at the trial. Moreover, in this case it is clear that there has been no mistake."

The three appeal judges spoke in whispers and Lord Hewart then told Sir Terence that his presence was no longer required. Charlotte Bryant, dressed in a neat blue dress and wearing a blue hat, listened calmly as her fate was being decided. She was the first woman in many years to be present at her own appeal.

She stood to hear it dismissed and only the paleness of her face gave any indication of the pressures bearing down upon her. She nodded gravely, turned and walked quietly and without assistance from the court. Maybe she had anticipated this verdict; for on the previous day, she had written to her son Ernest, "Think of me as last I was. I am thinking of you always."

Mr. D.N. Pritt, who was both a King's Counsellor and a Member of Parliament, asked the Home Secretary Sir John Simon whether he would consider introducing amending legislation to ensure that verdicts based on mistaken evidence should be subject to inquiry on appeal.

Sir John Simon replied, "I have ascertained from the Lord Chief Justice that he and the other judges sitting in the Court of Appeal proceeded on the assumption that this item of evidence was mistaken. I have also spoken to the trial judge, Mr. Justice MacKinnon, whose view was that the findings of Professor Bone did not affect in any way the validity of the jury's findings. The Judges of the Court of Criminal Appeal came to the conclusion, even on the assumption that Dr. Roche Lynch had been wrong, that the other evidence against Mrs. Bryant was so strong as to rule out any miscarriage of justice. And after most careful examination, I have reached the same view."

Officialdom was closing ranks and Mr. Casswell was furious and yet helpless to help his client further. He was seated in the Strangers' Gallery at the House of Commons when Sir John Simon made that statement and later he would admit, "Its contents staggered me."

He was still smarting from Lord Hewart's testily worded dismissal of the new scientific evidence as "objectionable". He also considered that Sir Terence O'Connor should have intervened to underline the seriousness of Dr. Roche Lynch's "dreadful blunder" which he had admitted privately.

Meanwhile Charlotte had been returned to the death cell at Exeter Prison and found at least one true friend in the form of Father Barney of the Church of the Sacred Heart. He built a temporary altar in her cell so that they could pray together and cancelled his holiday to make sure that she wouldn't feel abandoned in her desperate days of need.

While in Sherborne Police Station, she had been allowed to play with her children for a short while. But four months had gone by since then and she hadn't seen them again. She refused to see them in the condemned cell and told her solicitor, Mr. Christopher Arrow, "I would love to see Ernie and Lily. But I can't be cruel to them. I'm afraid they will never forget the Dorchester trial, and visiting me here would only make things worse."

Arrow later recalled how she had wept after making this decision to deny herself the pleasure of embracing her children in a last farewell. Then she had suggested, "I could see my baby" . . . but once again she decided against this.

The newspapers were much concerned about the fate of Charlotte's children. There were rumours that they would either be sent to a Catholic institution or to their grandmother in Ireland. This prompted Mrs. Violet Van der Elst, the premier campaigner against the death penalty, to announce that she was launching a fund for the children of murderers and their victims. She contributed fifty thousand pounds, a considerable sum in that day and age, to start it.

While waiting for death, Charlotte was learning to read and write. But although she was making surprisingly rapid progress, she decided to dictate her moving message to the sovereign: "Mighty King. Have pity on your lowly, afflicted subject. Don't let them kill me on Wednesday. From the brink of the cold, dark grave I, a poor helpless woman, ask you not to let them kill me. I am innocent."

This message addressed to King Edward VIII was her last despairing effort to save herself. And we will never know whether the King would have been moved enough to intervene. For he was never shown the letter. Instead it was diverted directly to the Home Secretary who had already stated his views on the matter in the House of Commons.

Charlotte's solicitor felt that a terrible injustice was being done and was unflagging in his efforts to save her. He wanted a new trial where fresh witnesses could be called. He persuaded Sir Stafford Cripps, Member of Parliament for East Bristol, to make a formal application for such a trial. And presumably as a result of this, the Home Secretary spoke to Professor Bone on the day before the execution. There is no written record of that conversation, but later that same day Sir Stafford Cripps received the Home Secretary's written answer in the

House of Commons. Sir John Simon saw no reason for interfering with the course of justice. There was to be no reprieve.

Charlotte's last hours were spent praying alongside the steadfast Father Barney. The authorities were worried that there could be a demonstration outside the prison, so they brought the time of the execution forward one hour. At eight o'clock on the morning of July 15, 1936, she was taken from her cell, supported by two warders as the chaplain intoned the service for the dead. She was said to have endured those last fearful moments bravely.

On the following Sunday, Father Barney told his congregation, "Shed no tears for Charlotte Bryant. She met her end with Christian fortitude and had the great consolation of a very thorough repentance. She had made her peace with God."

But despite the hours they had spent together, she had never confessed. On the contrary, she insisted right to the very end that she was totally innocent of her husband's murder. She did tell her solicitor, the faithful Mr. Arrow, that she'd bought the weed-killer; but again she had denied ever giving this to the unfortunate Fred.

The day after she died, Mary Frances Creighton and Everett Appelgate met their end in the electric chair at Sing Sing Prison in the United States. Mary Creighton had admitted poisoning Appelgate's wife with arsenic in 1935. It was an account of this case that Mrs. Ostler claimed to have read to Charlotte one night in the cottage. And the suggestion put to the jury was that this had given Charlotte the idea of poisoning her own husband.

Two days after she'd been hanged, her children were adopted by the Dorset County Council. And Mr. Arrow shared out her entire worldly goods. . . five shillings and eightpence halfpenny. . . amongst these five children.

It was a sad and disturbing case and it is very unlikely that any modern jury would have convicted her on the evidence presented before that Dorchester court.

Everything was circumstantial and there wasn't a jot of direct evidence to support the charge.

It was generally accepted that Fred Bryant had been poisoned by one of the two women in the cottage that night, his wife Charlotte or Lucy Ostler. And the Crown's decision to charge Charlotte and use Mrs. Ostler as the chief prosecution witness created a strange situation. For by so doing, they had given Mrs. Ostler good cause for hoping to see her former friend found guilty. Because if Charlotte wasn't guilty, Mrs. Ostler was. So much of her most damaging evidence had to be regarded with a degree of suspicion, due to this vested interest. It also had to be deemed possible that the two women had been acting in collusion. It could be argued that Charlotte was the more probable suspect but murder verdicts are seldom returned on the basis of probability.

The Crown had alleged that Charlotte poisoned her husband so that she would be free to marry Parsons; but this motive always sounded thin. Charlotte had once described Fred Bryant as "the most unjealous man I've ever known." No one had heard him object even once to Parson's presence in his wife's bed. At times, he even seemed to encourage their affair.

It had been alleged that, due to a war wound, he was no longer capable of satisfying Charlotte's very considerable sexual demands, and was therefore quite happy for Parsons to undertake that chore. In court, Parsons had stated that Charlotte propositioned him, saying, "I think I shall be a widow soon, Bill. When that happens will you marry me?" Parsons testified that she asked him this question several times and that on each occasion he answered, "No." He had, after all, already left the cottage and departed for pastures new. The remark "I think I shall be a widow soon" doesn't necessarily have any sinister context, for she was talking about an obviously sick man – a man whom the insurance agent had described as "one who had not much longer to live." So if Charlotte really was a murderess, just what could have been her motive?

With Fred's death, she would almost certainly have lost the cottage and seemingly gained nothing.

But the real question about the trial of Charlotte Bryant has to be: would the jury still have found her guilty if it had been shown clearly to them that the evidence of a respected forensic scientist was wrong on such a key point?

Lord Hewart's refusal to listen to Professor Bone's evidence coupled with Sir John Simon's refusal to order a retrial did little to advance the cause of the British legal system. And Mr. Casswell was one of many eminent lawyers who considered that Charlotte Bryant had suffered an injustice.

She leaves behind a mystery that may never be solved – the missing word in that tantalising message: "It's all ......'s fault I'm here. I listened to the tales I was told. But I have not long now and I will be out of all my troubles. God bless my children."

Could that missing word have been either Lucy's or Bill's? What were the tales she'd been told? What did the message really mean? And why did the prison governor blank out the name?

Killarney Kate, a girl who'd once dreamed of streets paved with gold, took the answers with her to that "cold, dark grave."

# 27

# THE YIELDING ROPE

*"You'll make me laugh at you directly."*
*James O'Connor interrupting Mr. Justice Brett, as he was*
*pronouncing the death sentence.*

The moment when the learned judge donned the black
cap must have come to the prisoners in the dock like
something out of the most horrendous nightmare.
Newspapers during the hanging days were apt to use stock
phrases to describe such moments. . . "the condemned
man turned pale". . . "the prisoner staggered and almost
fell." And it's true that in some cases, the convicted
murderer or murderess had to be supported on the way to
the cells below. The tragic Irish beauty Charlotte Bryant,
for instance, was in a state of near collapse. But the vast
majority endured this grim ritual with surprising calmness.
Maybe they had already accepted the inevitable. After all,
very few capital murderers put up much of a defence. And
maybe the unreal atmosphere of a courtroom with the
robed and bewigged men of the law belonging to some
bygone age took away some of the reality.

Nevertheless the remarks made by condemned men in
that awesome moment are worth recalling. A few would
protest their innocence to the very end. The powerful
Alfred Bostock, killer of 'Miss Untouchable', took the
opportunity to tell the judge, "I am innocent and if the

dead girl's lips could only speak, they would tell you the same."

Said Albert Hall, the man who smiled too much, "My Lord, I am not guilty of this crime. It is a terrible crime, I admit, but I am not guilty of it."

Lawrence Fowler, whose gang had terrorised the city of Sheffield, "If Jock Plommer's wife had told the truth, this court would know I was innocent."

On a sadder note there was the appeal of the dim-witted Irishman Pat Morley which summed up his character so neatly, "You see, yur riverance, it was only a little revolver. I hadn't thought the trigger would go off."

Then there was the bombshell delivered by the pint-sized Louie Calvert who, when asked whether she had anything to say before sentence was passed, replied simply, "Yes, sir, I'm pregnant."

The ex-soldier Bert Salisbury, when asked the same question, replied politely, "No, thank you, sir."

Many displayed a true sense of style and none more so than Pat McKenna, speaking of the wife he had stabbed to death in a fit of jealousy, "She was as good a woman as was ever married and tied to a man."

Fred Ballington, a quiet man, looked towards his family and mouthed the word, "Goodbye".

William Wardell, the gigolo, gave a mock bow to an attractive woman in the public gallery.

Charlie Peace smiled as though he hadn't a care in the whole wide world.

And the eccentric Eric Rothwell Holt turned to the prison governor and said, "Well, that's over. I hope my tea won't be late."

Most of the condemned gave the judges a respect they didn't always deserve. But James O'Connor proved to be the great exception. On a September afternoon in 1873, he was tried at the Liverpool Assizes and found guilty of the wilful murder of Patrick Garrow, a fellow Irishman.

Mr. Justice Brett, one of the more kindly judges, had donned the black cap somewhat reluctantly and was endeavouring to give him as much consolation as lay in his power. In a sympathetic voice, he said that he understood how basically good men could be led astray by the passions. . . even to the point where in a moment of near madness, they committed the most heinous crime of all, the murder of a fellow human being. Gently he begged O'Connor to repent while there was still time and make his peace with Heaven. . .

He was about to say more when O'Connor interrupted, saying scornfully, "You'll make me laugh at you directly."

There was a stunned silence in the courtroom. Then the judge continued, but now his voice was stern and harsh, devoid of pity. "And the sentence of the Law is that you be taken from this court to the place from whence you came, and thence to a place of lawful execution, and that there you be hanged by the neck until you be dead, and after your execution that your body be buried within the precincts of the gaol in which you shall last have been confined prior to your execution. And may the Lord have mercy on your soul."

To this the chaplain reverently added, "Amen."

O'Connor was a blue-eyed charmer, a ladykiller with a penchant for stealing the wives of other men. But he had fallen heavily for a lissom lovely named Sheila Shears and then lost her to another charmer, Patrick Garrow. Driven on by jealousy, he had stabbed Garrow to death.

A young journalist had been in court to see O'Connor sentenced and has left a remarkable record of the events that followed. This is his report published many years later:

"The colossal cheek of the prisoner so impressed me that I determined to be one of the little gathering of spectators who in those days were admitted to witness executions. Being well known in the town, I had not much difficulty in obtaining the necessary card of admission from the chairman of the visiting justices, and on a bleak morning I presented myself at the door of

Kirkdale Prison. A warder admitted me, in company with five other press men, and we were shown into a yard, at one corner of which stood the gallows. It was a permanent structure built of wood, the front being draped in black.

"In the cold we waited, shivering, fearing to witness the very tragedy we had come to see. On the scaffold was a young man, fussing about, examining this, testing that. It was Marwood, then only an assistant hangman.

"Presently we heard a gate swing back with a sudden clang, the sound of footsteps, and a voice exclaiming, "Ad Dominum cum tribularer clamavi; et exaudivit me" (I called on the Lord when I was in trouble and He heard me), the opening passages of the Roman Catholic service for the dead.

"Nearer and nearer came the sounds, the steady tramp of footsteps being mingled with the piteous prayer, "Eternal rest give unto him, oh Lord." Then a little procession emerged from the doorway. The robed priest walked directly in front of the condemned, a bound figure – surely the saddest sight that man can gaze upon. Next hobbled an aged, palsied, trembling man – Calcraft, the official executioner. The fascination of the scene rivetted my gaze on the culprit. The impudent swagger which he maintained in court was gone; but the Irishman's cheeks were not blanched by fear.

"At the foot of the fatal tree, Father Bonte offered O'Connor a crucifix to kiss, which he did with evident devotion. I shuddered as Calcraft placed the rope around the victim's throat and drew it tight, and try as I would, I could not turn my eyes from the pitiful figure standing on the drop. The white-robed priest – last friend of the dying man on earth – read on.

"A crash! A thud! The end had come. No; the rope flies loosely in the air. What has happened?

"With a vault Father Bonte sprang into the pit, his priestly vestments flying in the wind. I followed him. Propped up against the wooden partition lay O'Connor, with broken rope around his neck, and the white cap over his eyes. The good cleric at once drew off the cap and loosened the noose, while he whispered words of consolation into the wretched felon's ear. But it was not to him that the condemned man turned. It was to me: seizing my arm with his two pinioned hands, he exclaimed, "I stood it bravely, didn't I? You will let me off now, won't you? Let me off, do."

"Think of the horror of that appeal. "You will let me off, won't you?" And there was no power to do so. "There to be hanged by the neck until you are dead," was the dread sentence, and the Law must be obeyed.

"The half-hanged man was supported by warders and taken behind the scaffold, while the other officials hurriedly procured a new rope, and then again he was placed in position. Calcraft pulled the lever, the drop fell, and James O'Connor was dead.

"Searching through my scrapbook the other day I came across the following lines, clipped from one of the Northern papers of the time, which express the popular feeling of Liverpool with regard to the horrid tragedy:

"Hanged by the neck till you be dead"
So peals the dreadful sentence, while shocked
Nature reels.

The Angels wept when primal man first fell:
And Heavenly Love rang Eden's passing bell.
But Hell's own fiends must point at and deride
The Christian Laws by which James O'Connor died.
"Vengeance is mine." Yet we usurp the brand
Already poised in God's avenging hand.
Man's life is sacred. Christ himself hath deigned
To wear the form which human sin hath stained.
It is no plea that men deserve to die:
"Thou shalt not kill" is thundered from the sky.
Though form and circumstance were ranged beside,
Connor, twice hung, was murdered ere he died.

Oh when will England, peerless, chiefest, best,

Call sense of feeling to her parent breast?
Mercy dictates the Gibbet should be hurled
Out from the confines of a Christian world.

Shame on the Laws which boast as their last hope
A palsied hangman and a yielding rope.